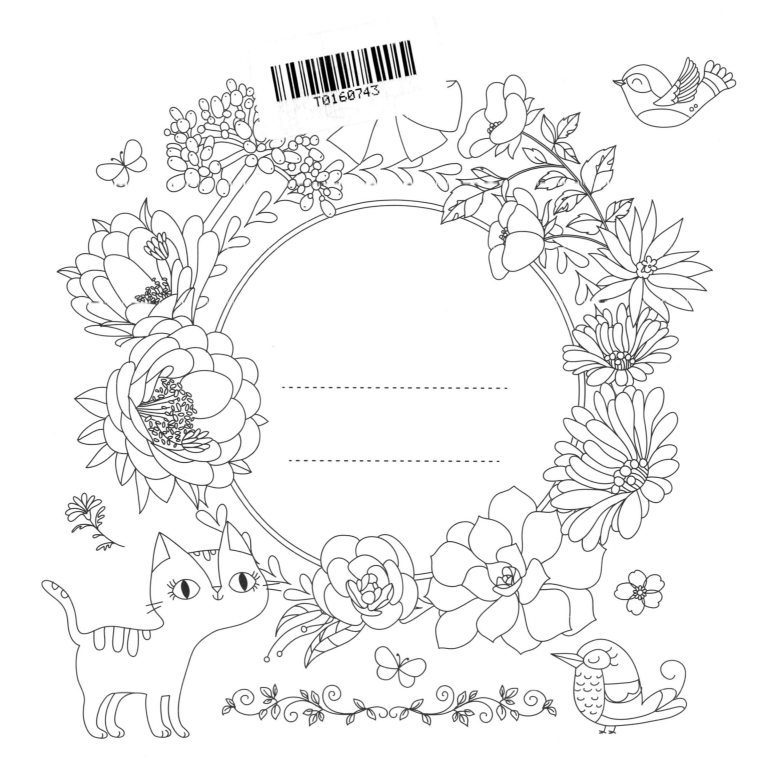

FRAME FANTASIA contains a beautiful collection of picture frames of many different styles and genres to colour in. But that is not all!
At the end of the book you will find a floral alphabet to copy or trace.
You can create a name, an inspiring phrase, or even a magic word!
This means you will be able to frame your favourite names or phrases as well as photographs and drawings. For decoration or giving away as a present.
There is also a picture frame template that you can duplicate in card, cardboard, foam core board or even balsa wood. With the template you can have as many frames as you want.
Your favourite thoughts and moments have finally found their perfect home.

MOMENTOS MÁGICOS ofrece una colección de bellísimos marcos para colorear de una gran variedad de estilos y tipologías. ¡Pero hay mucho más!
En las últimas páginas encontrarás un alfabeto floral para copiar o calcar. Puedes crear un nombre, una frase inspiradora, o una palabra mágica.
Así podrás enmarcar, además de fotografías o dibujos, tus frases o nombres especiales. Para decorar o regalar.
Al final del libro hay una plantilla de marco que puedes reproducir en cartulina, cartón, cartón pluma o incluso madera de balsa. Con la plantilla tendrás todos los marcos que quieras.
Por fin tus instantes y pensamientos favoritos ya tienen su espacio perfecto.

NATURE CADRÉE propose une collection de magnifiques cadres à colorier dans une grande variété de styles et typologies. Mais ce n'est pas tout!
Les dernières pages du livre renferment un alphabet floral que vous pourrez recopier ou décalquer pour créer un nom, une phrase qui vous inspire ou un mot magique!
Ainsi, vous pourrez encadrer non seulement vos photos et dessins, mais aussi les phrases et noms qui vous sont chers. Pour décorer ou pour offrir.
À la fin du livre, vous trouverez un gabarit de cadre que vous pourrez reproduire en bristol, en carton ou carton mousse, voire même en balsa. Avec le gabarit vous pourrez créer autant de cadres que vous voulez.
Vos moments de détente et de rêverie ont enfin trouvé un cadre idéal.

MOMENTI MAGICI offre una collezione di bellissime cornici da colorare, in una grande varietà di stili e modelli. Ma c'è molto di più!
Nelle ultime pagine, troverai un alfabeto floreale da copiare o ricalcare. Potrai creare un nome, una frase ispirata, o una parola magica.
In questo modo, potrai incorniciare, oltre a fotografie e disegni, anche le tue frasi preferite o quei nomi per te speciali. Per decorare o da regalare.
Alla fine del libro, troverai un modello di cornice che potrai riprodurre in cartoncino, cartone, carton plume o anche in legno di balsa. Con il modellino otterrai tutte le cornici che desideri.
Finalmente i tuoi momenti e pensieri prediletti troveranno il loro spazio ideale.

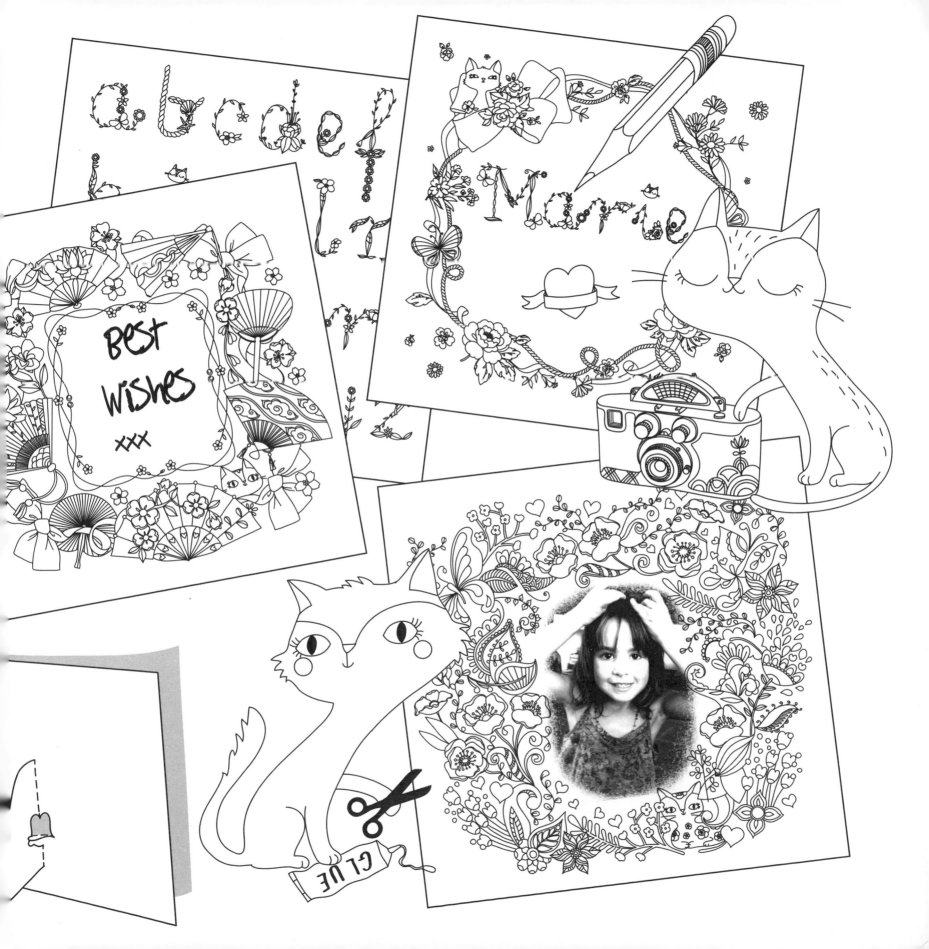

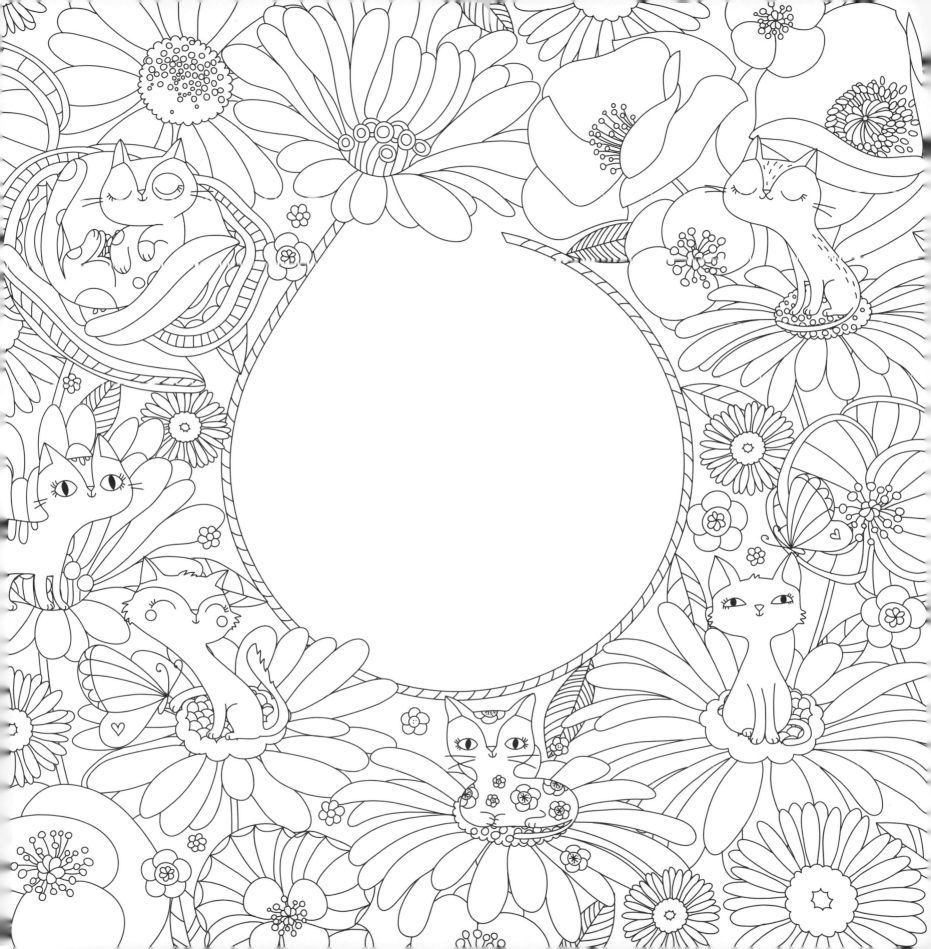

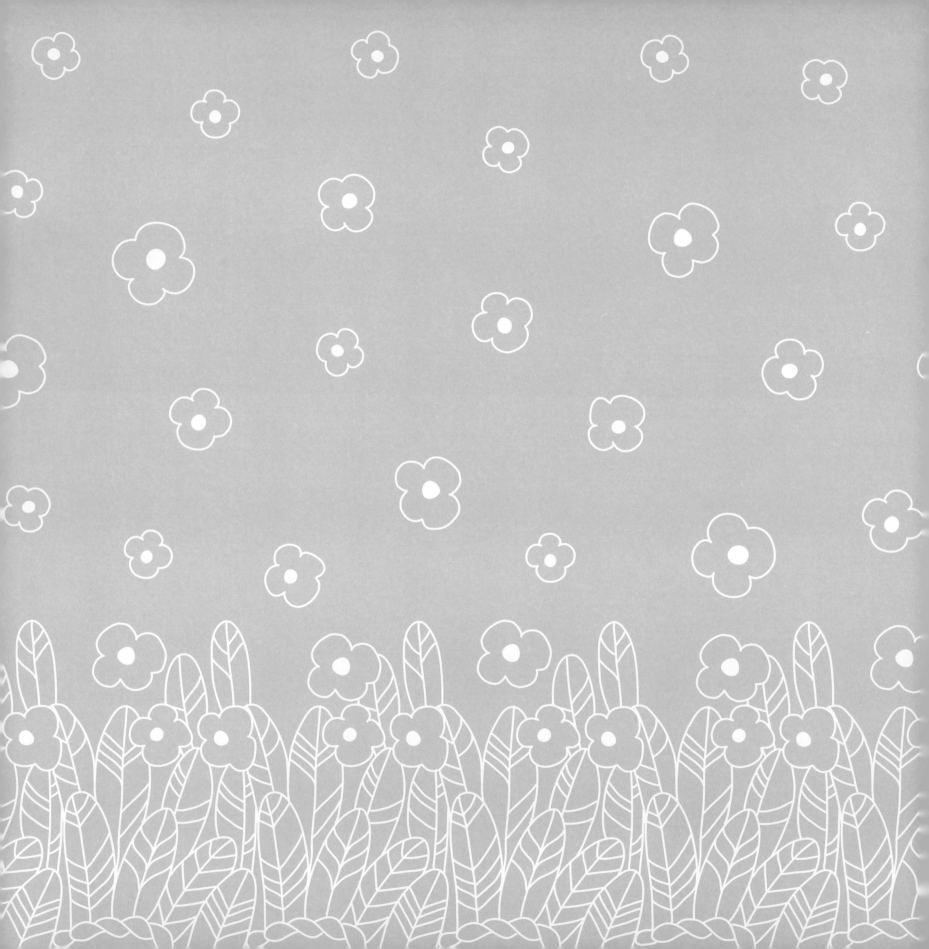

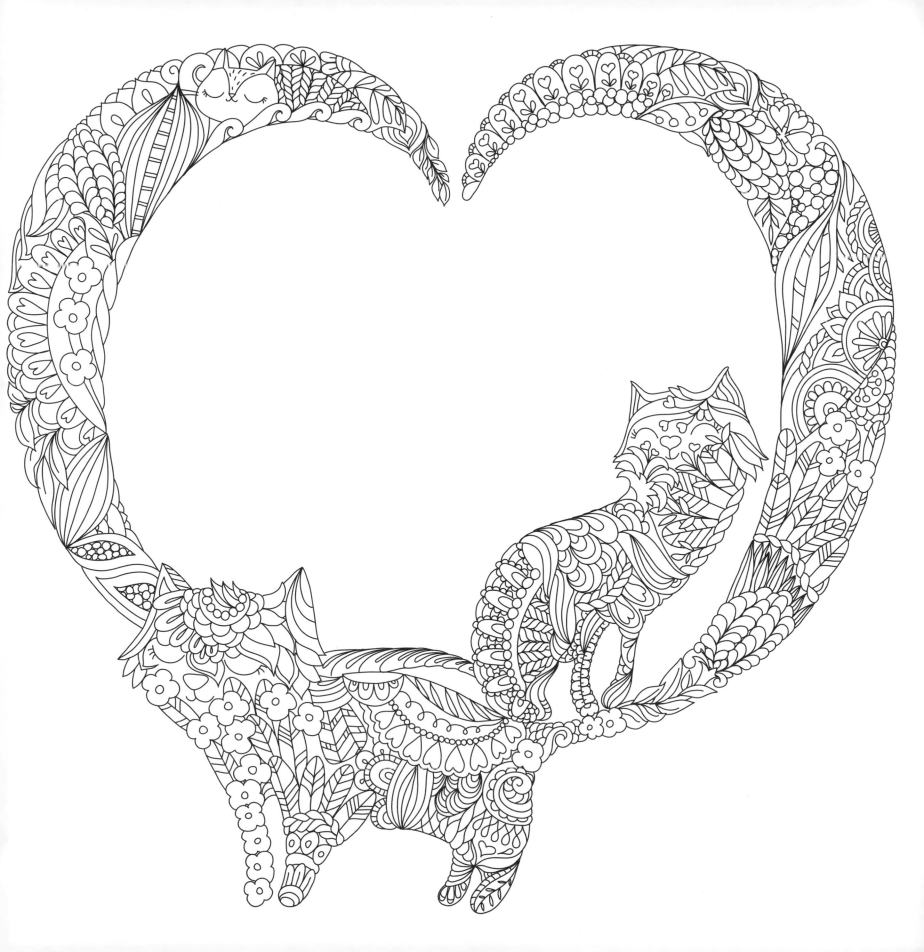

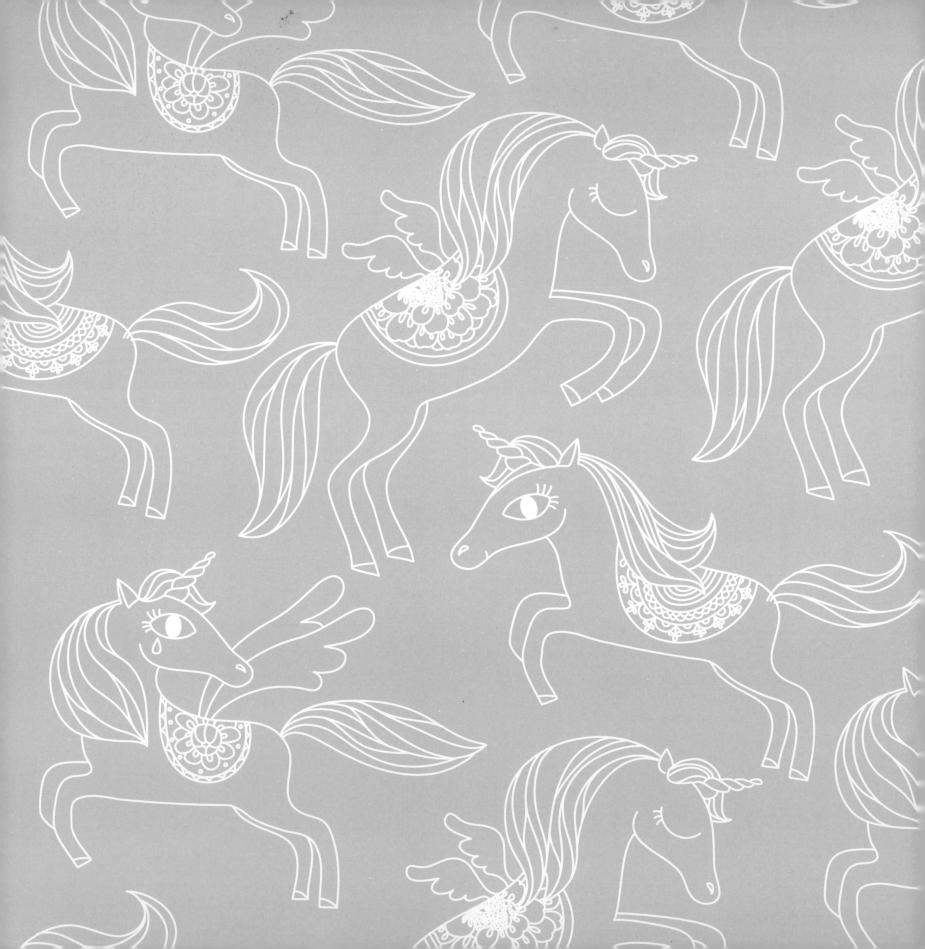

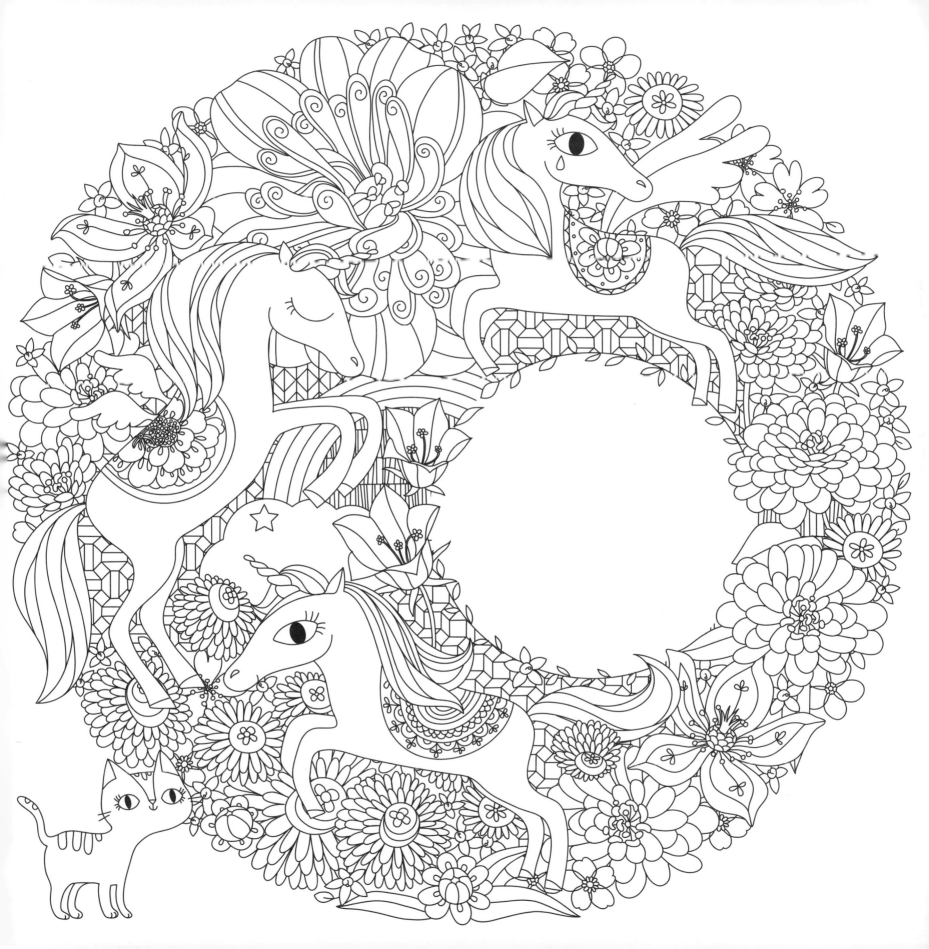

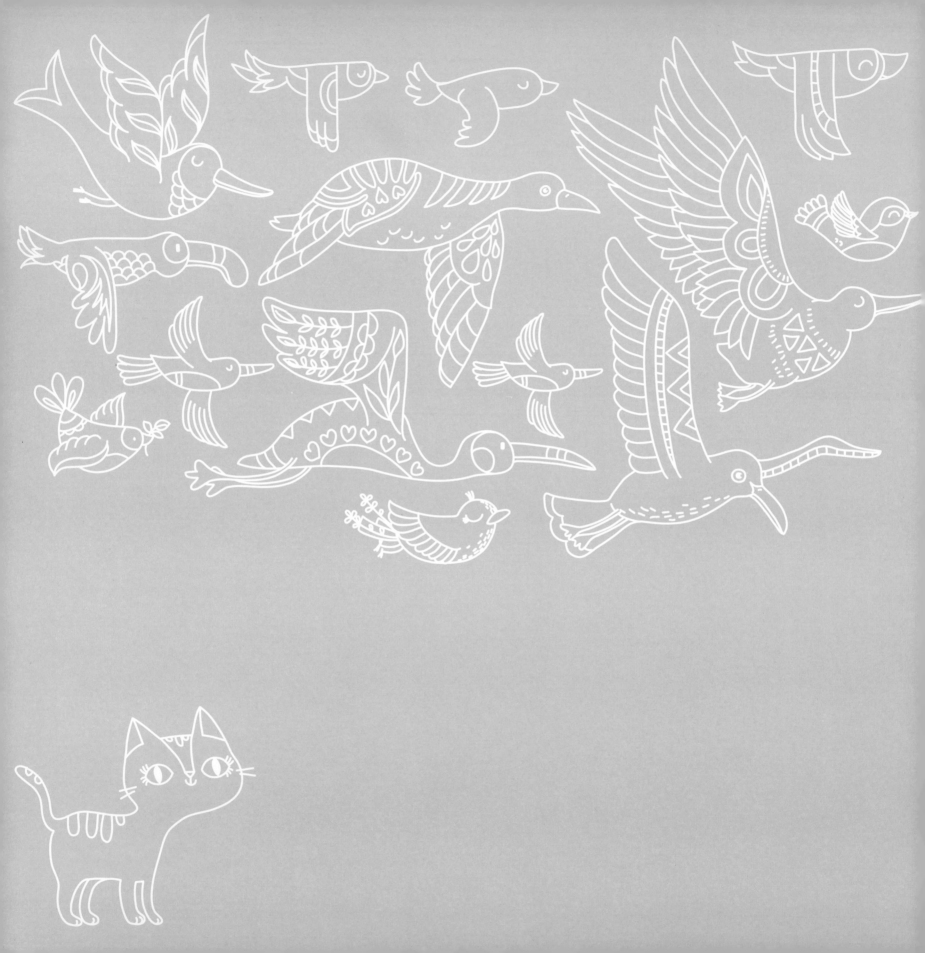

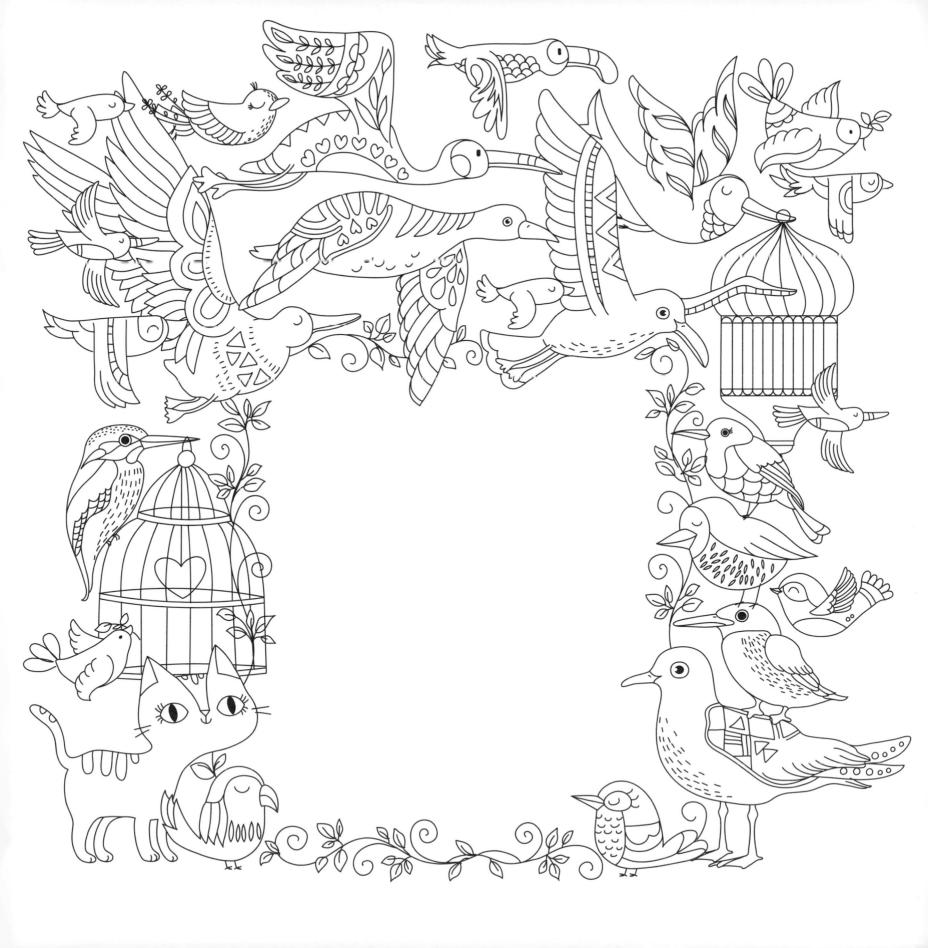

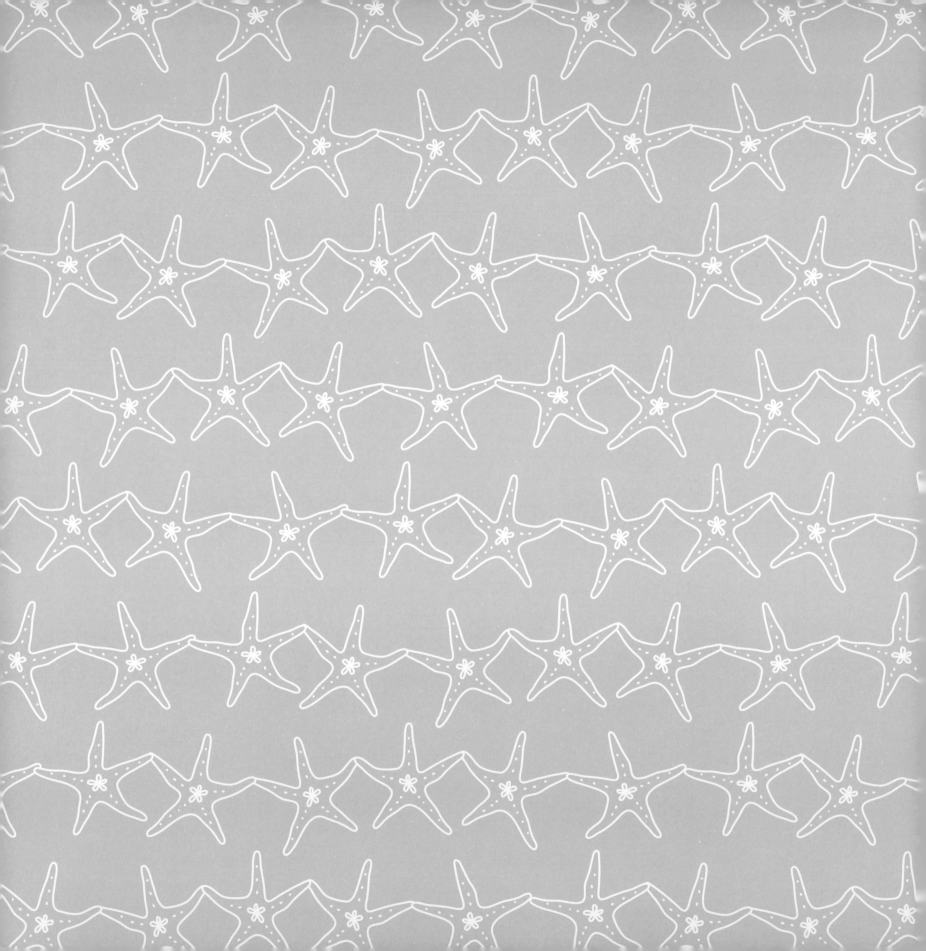

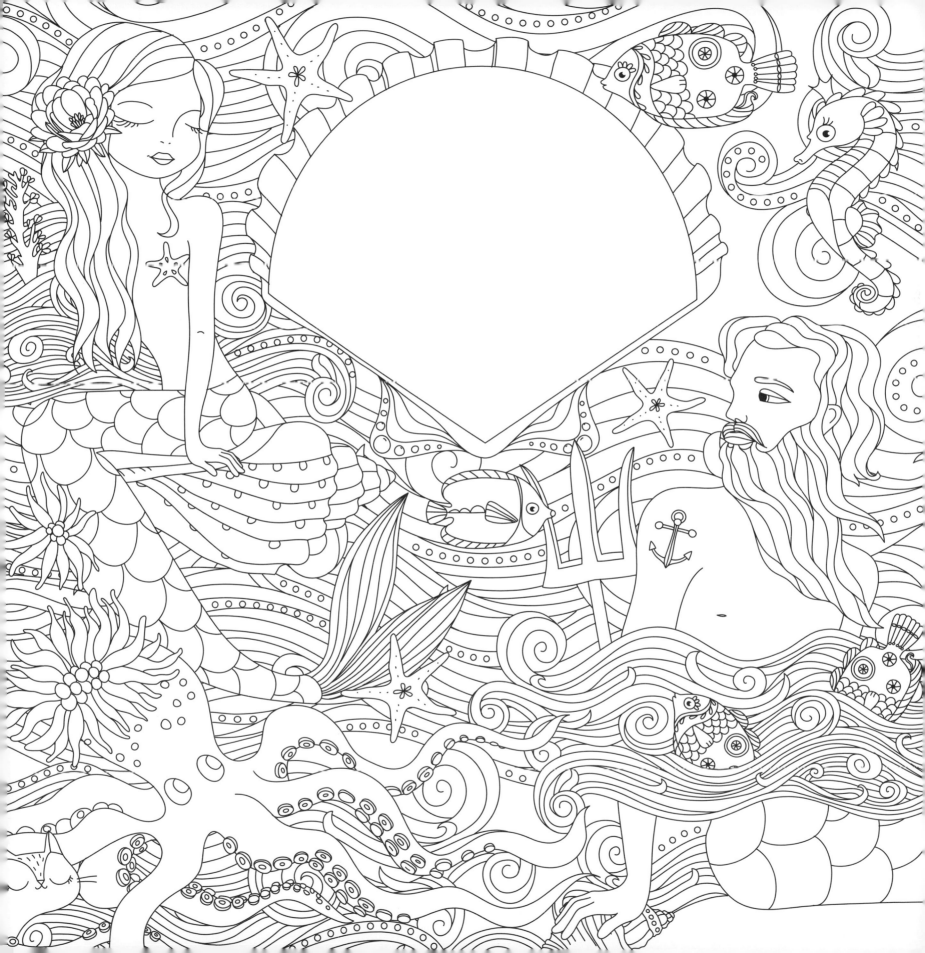

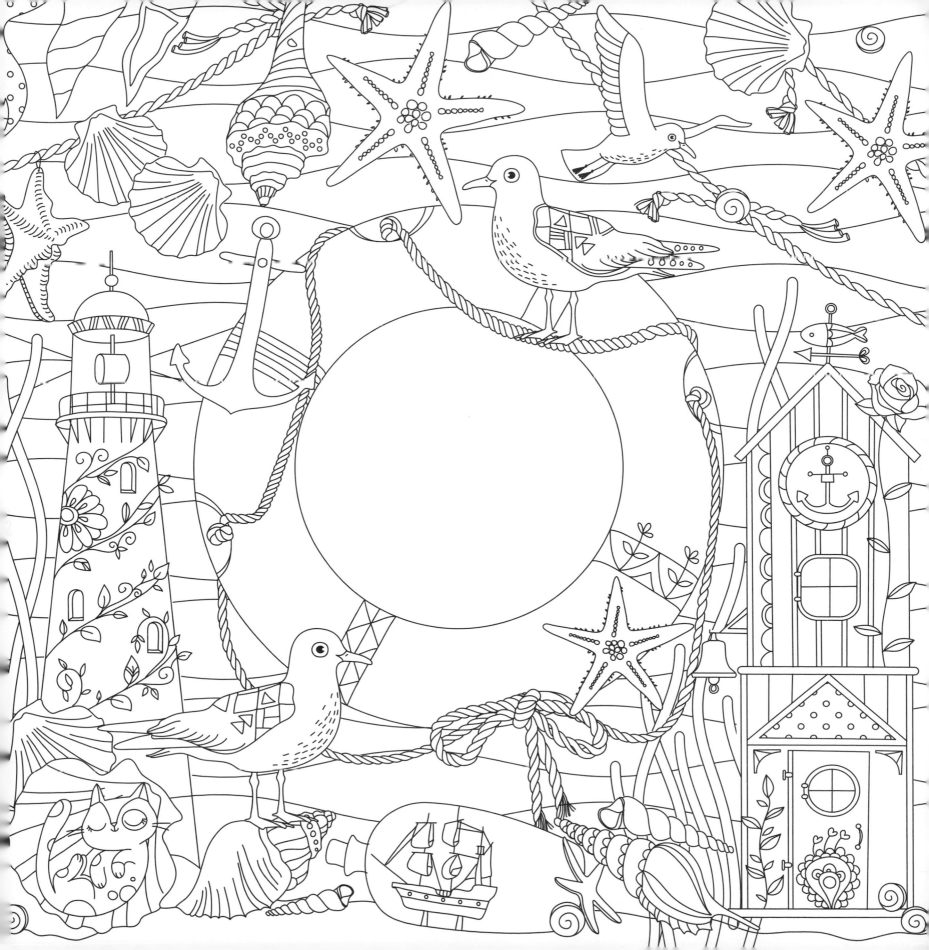

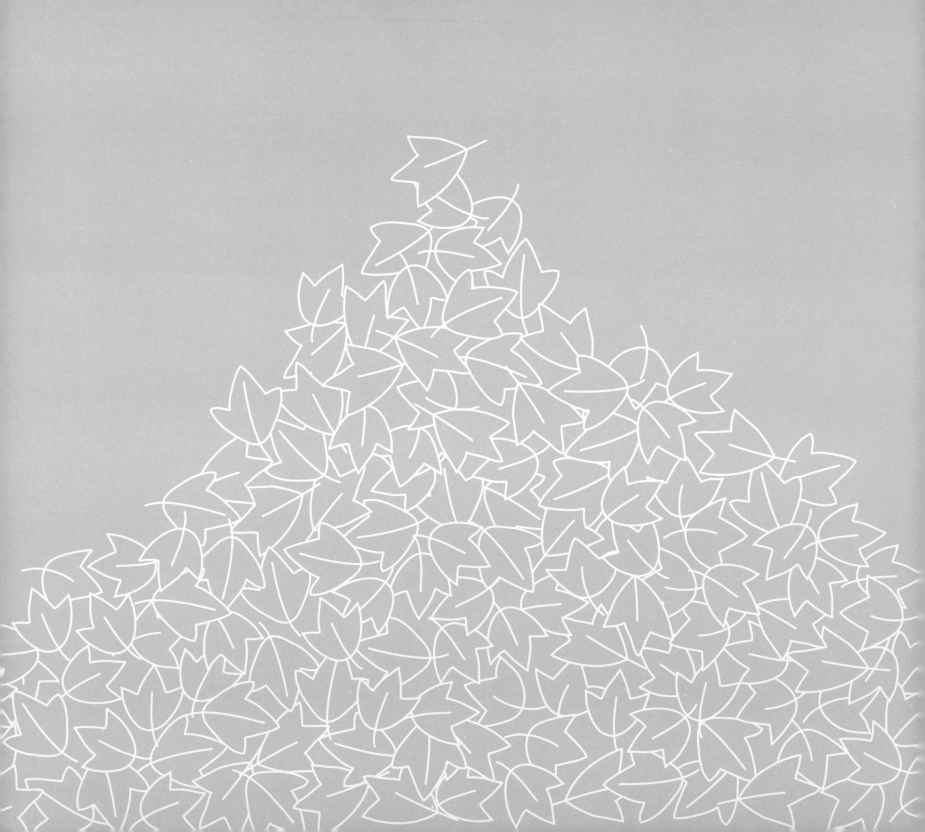

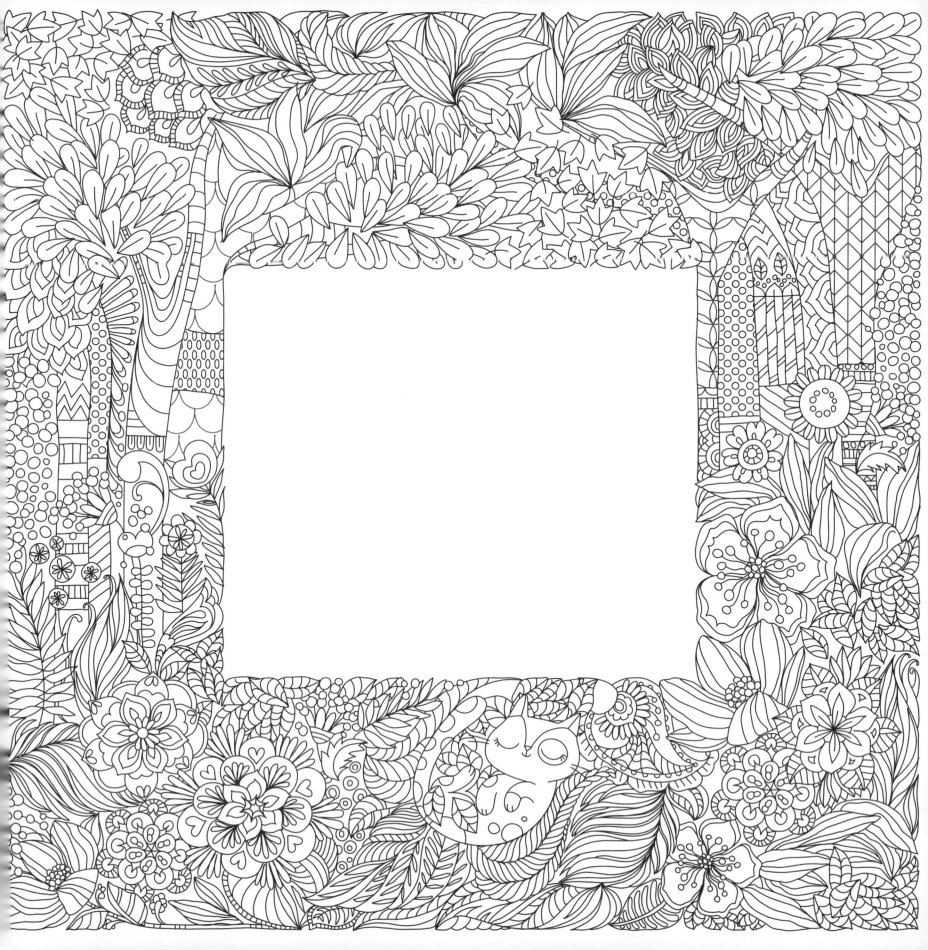

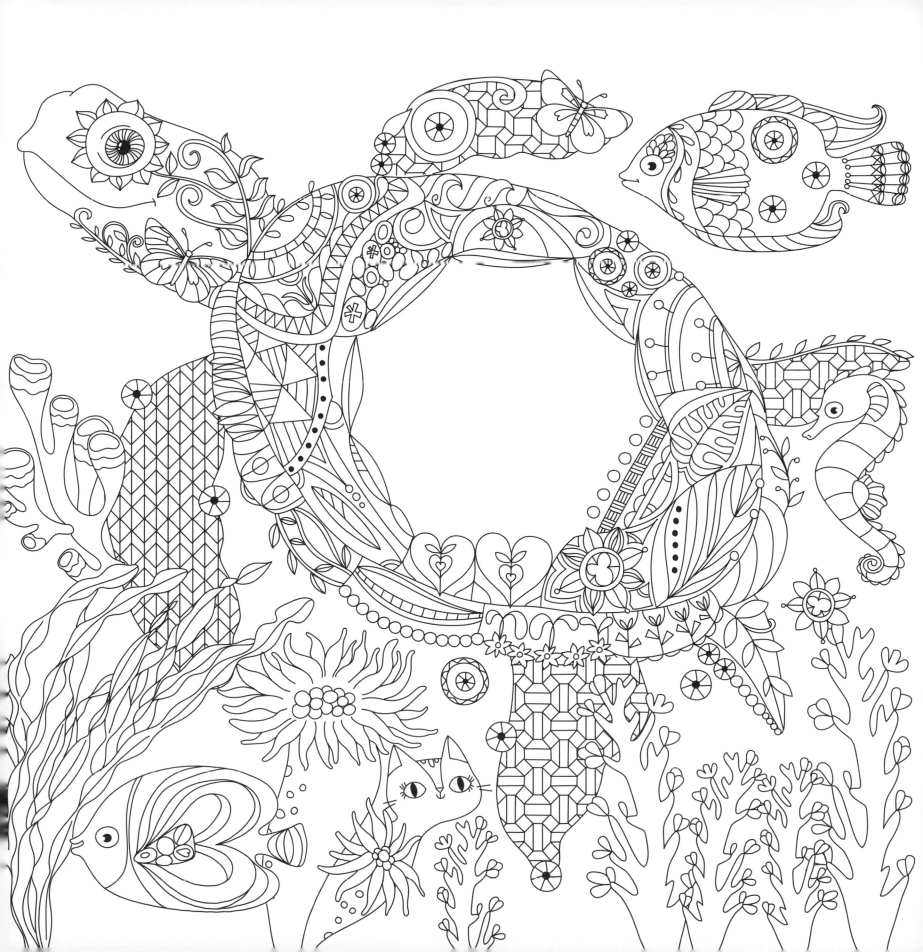

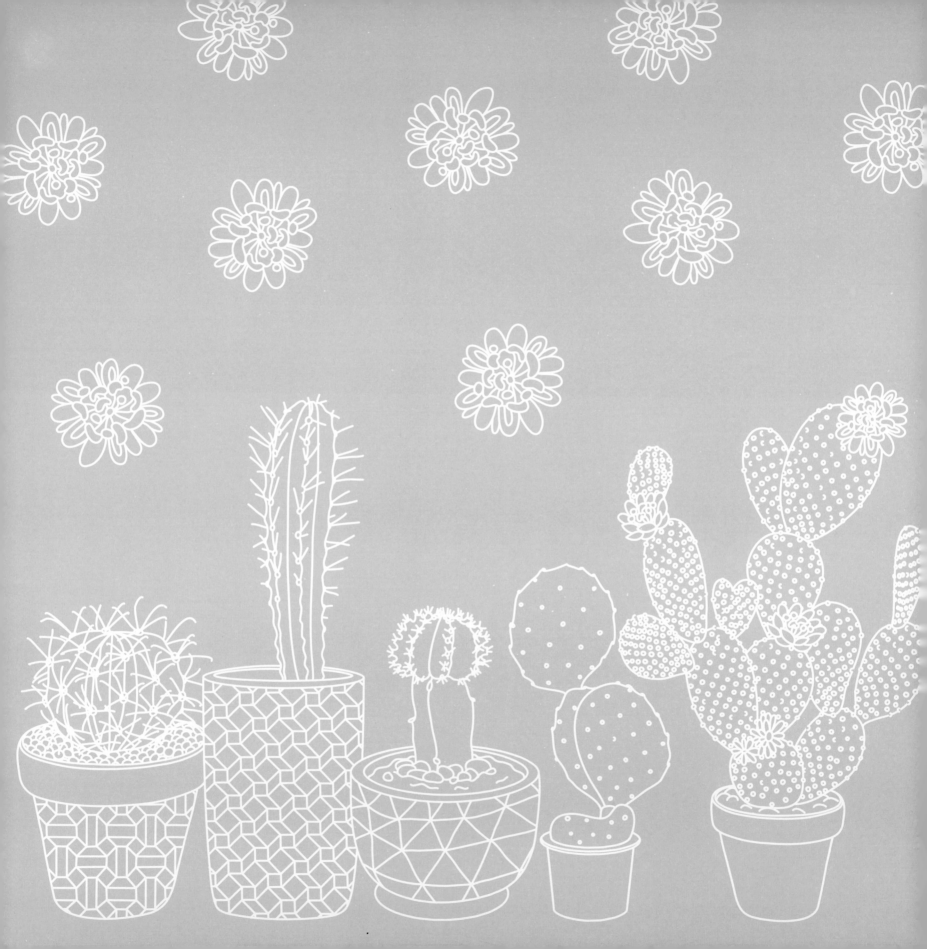

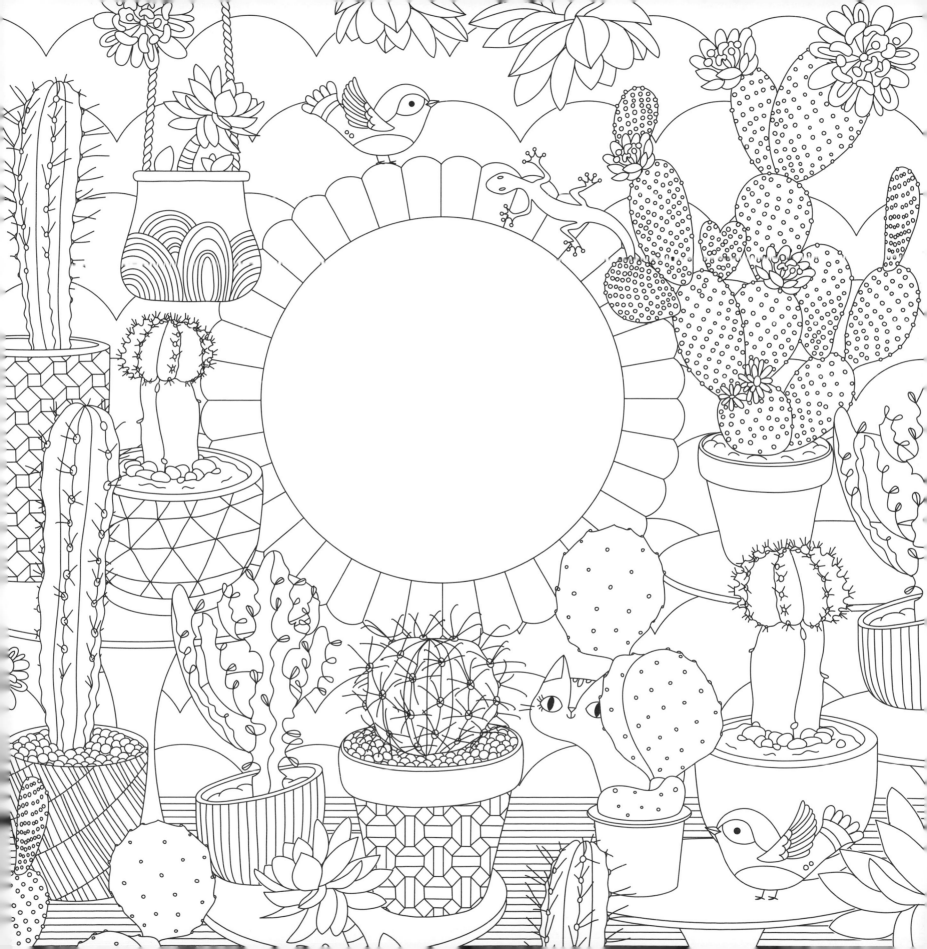

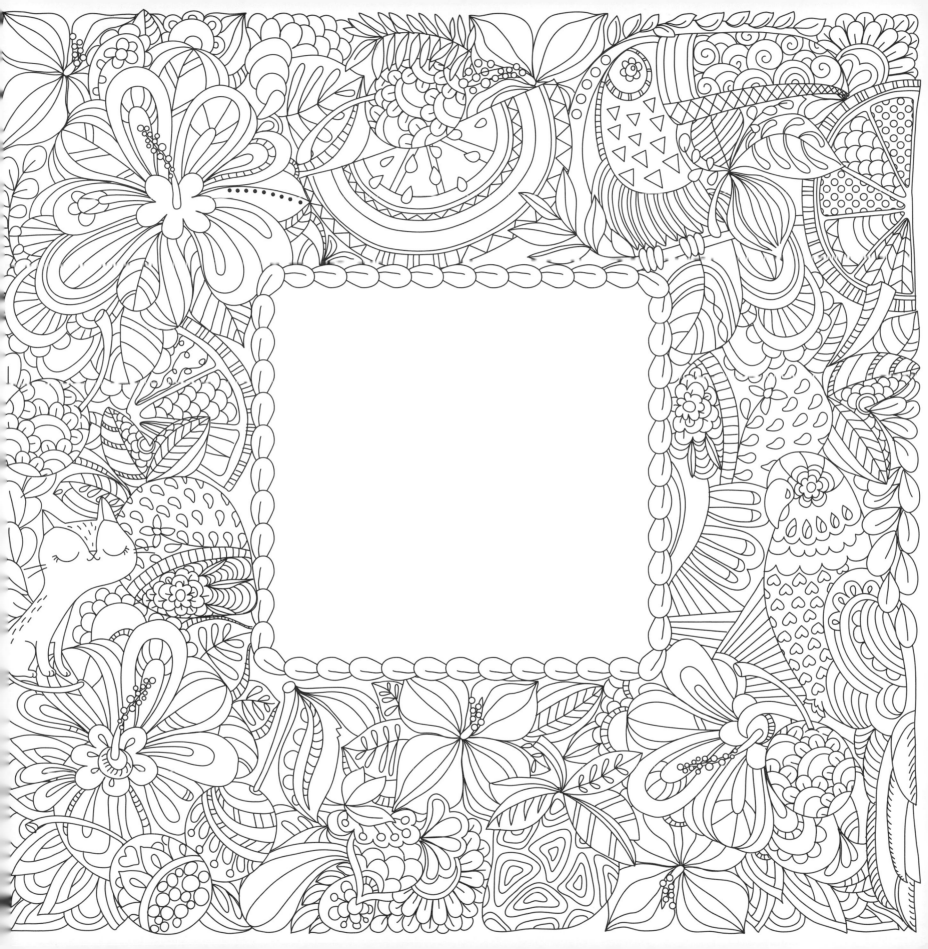

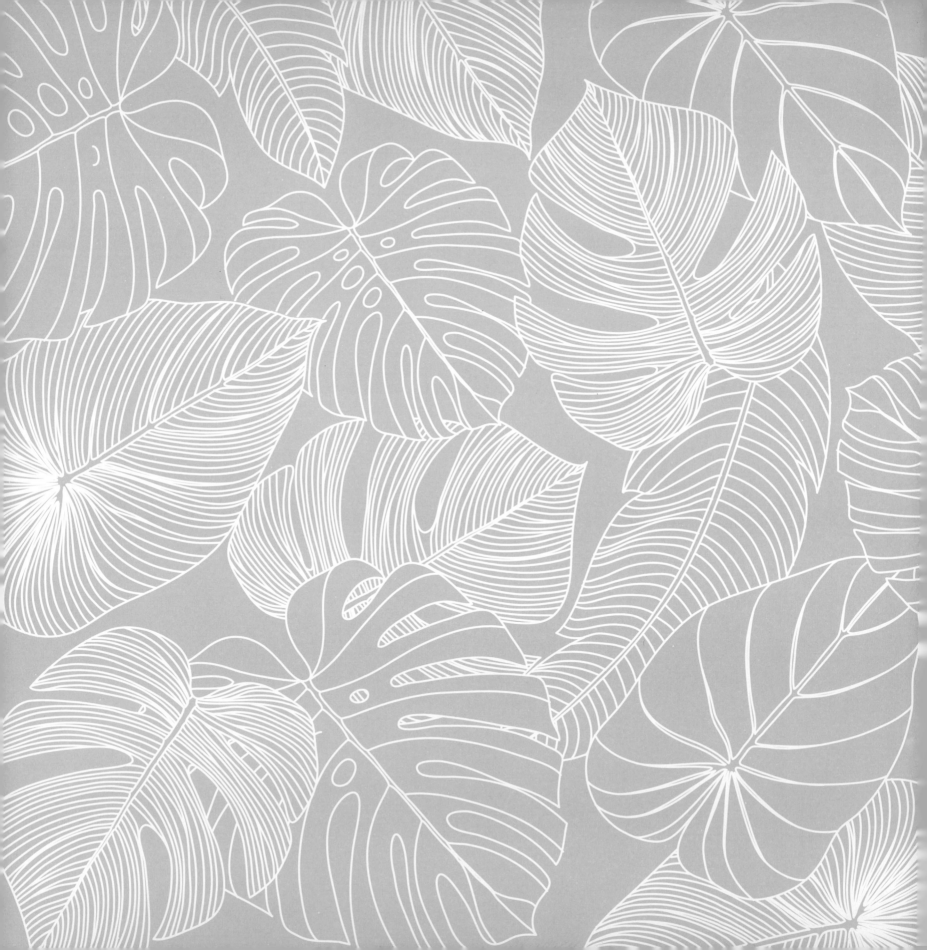

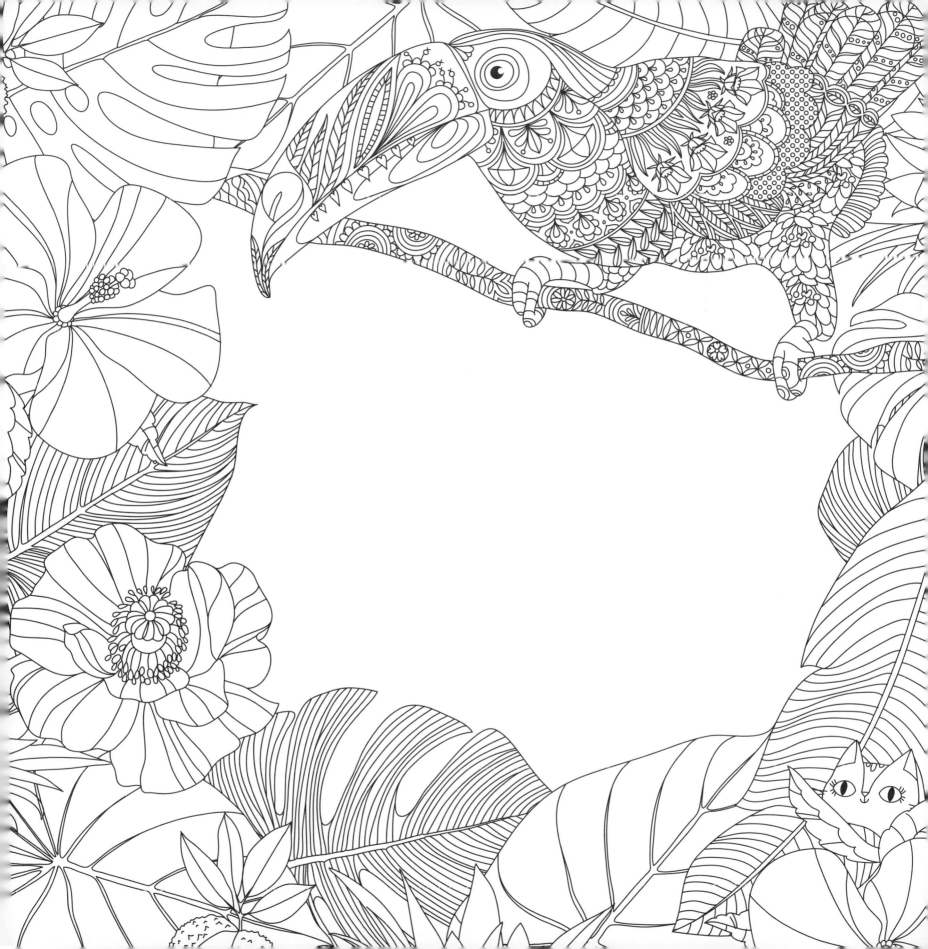

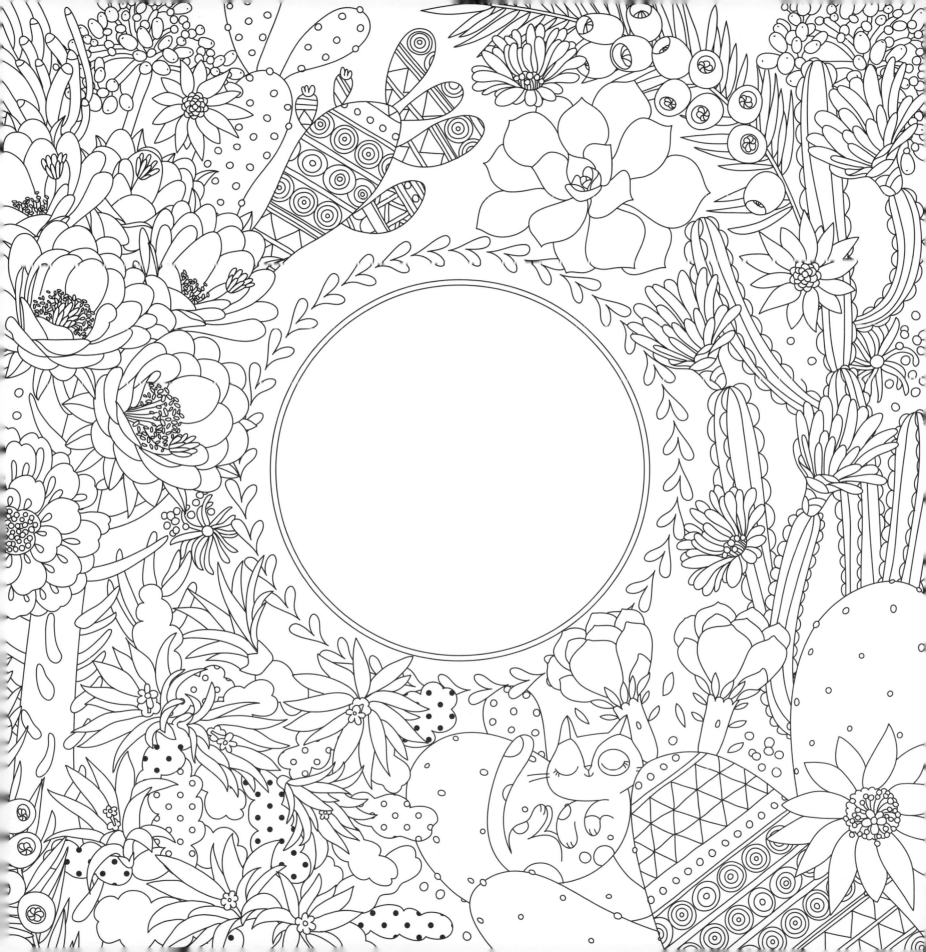

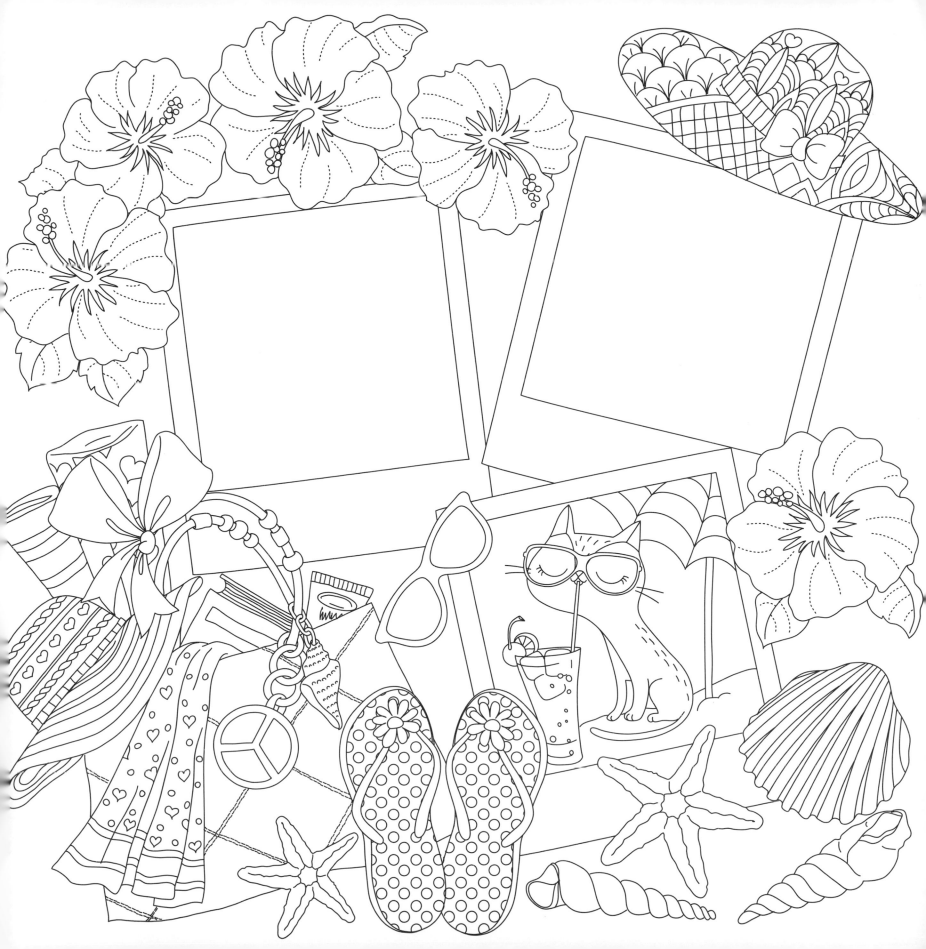

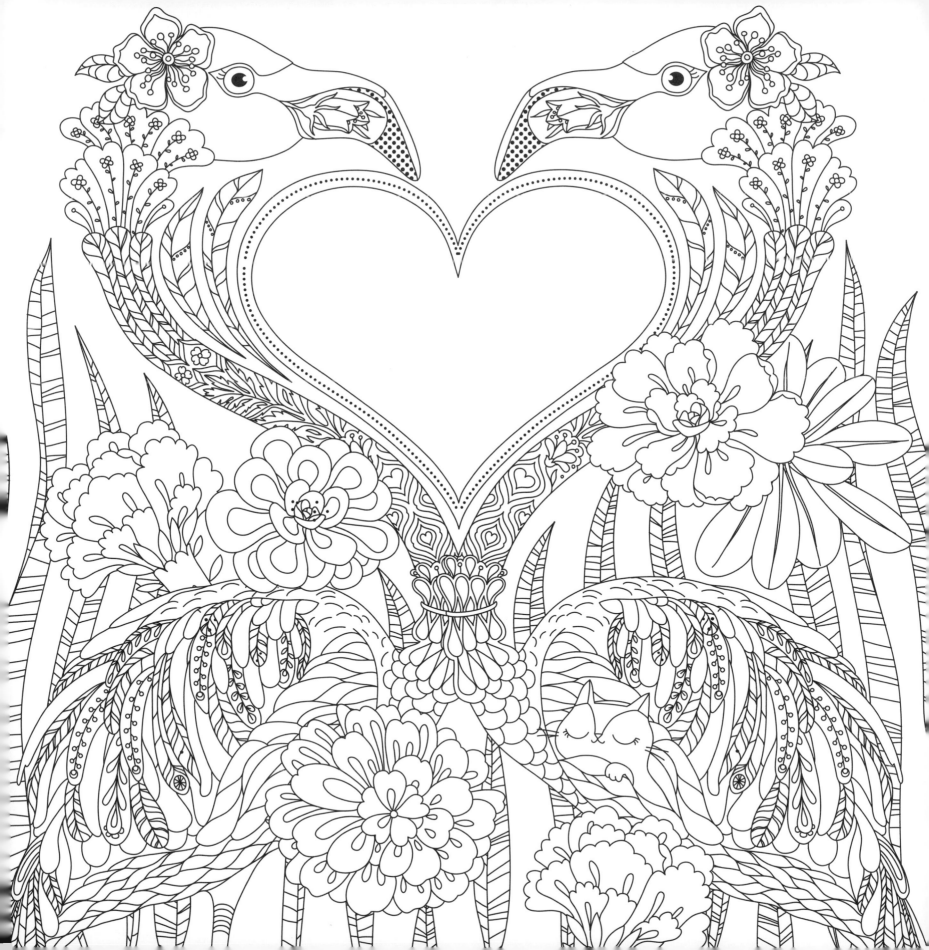

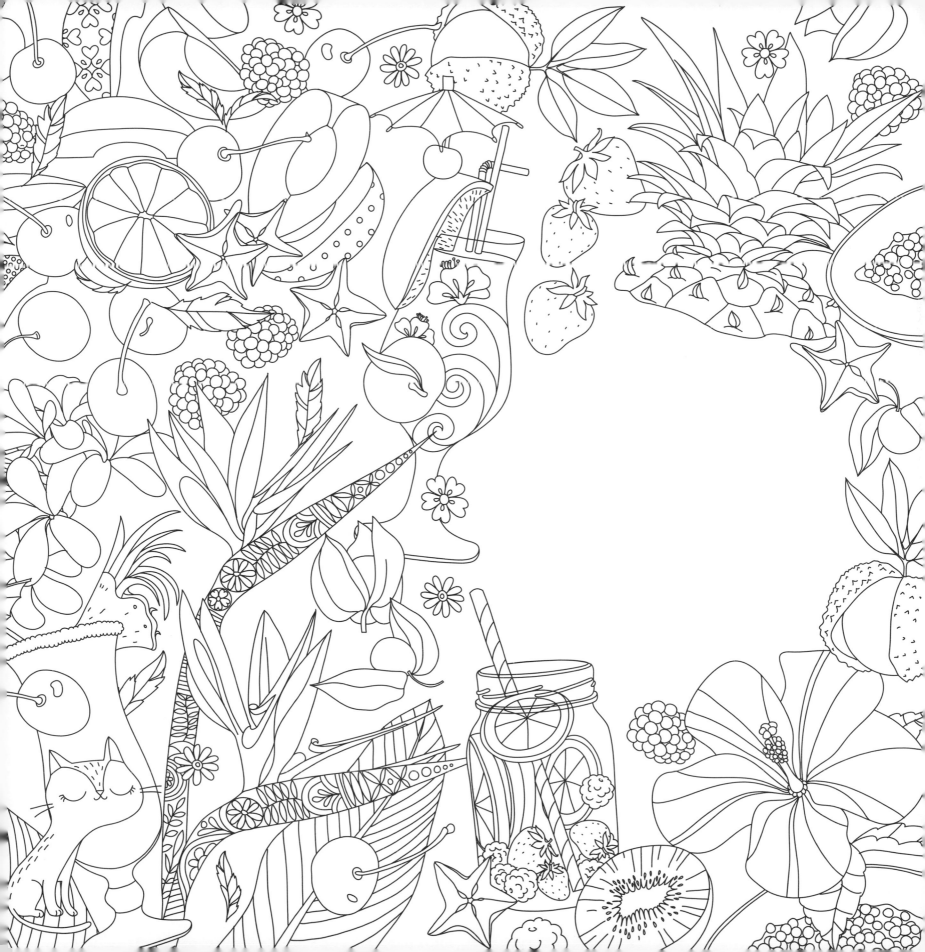

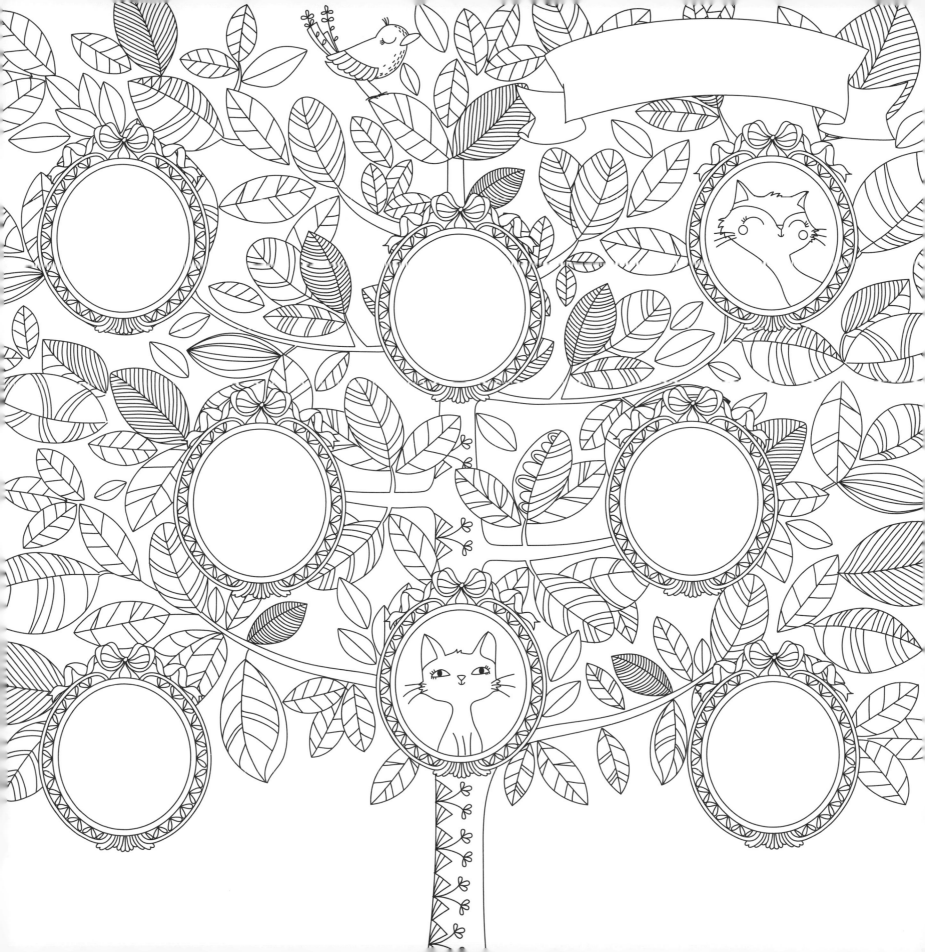

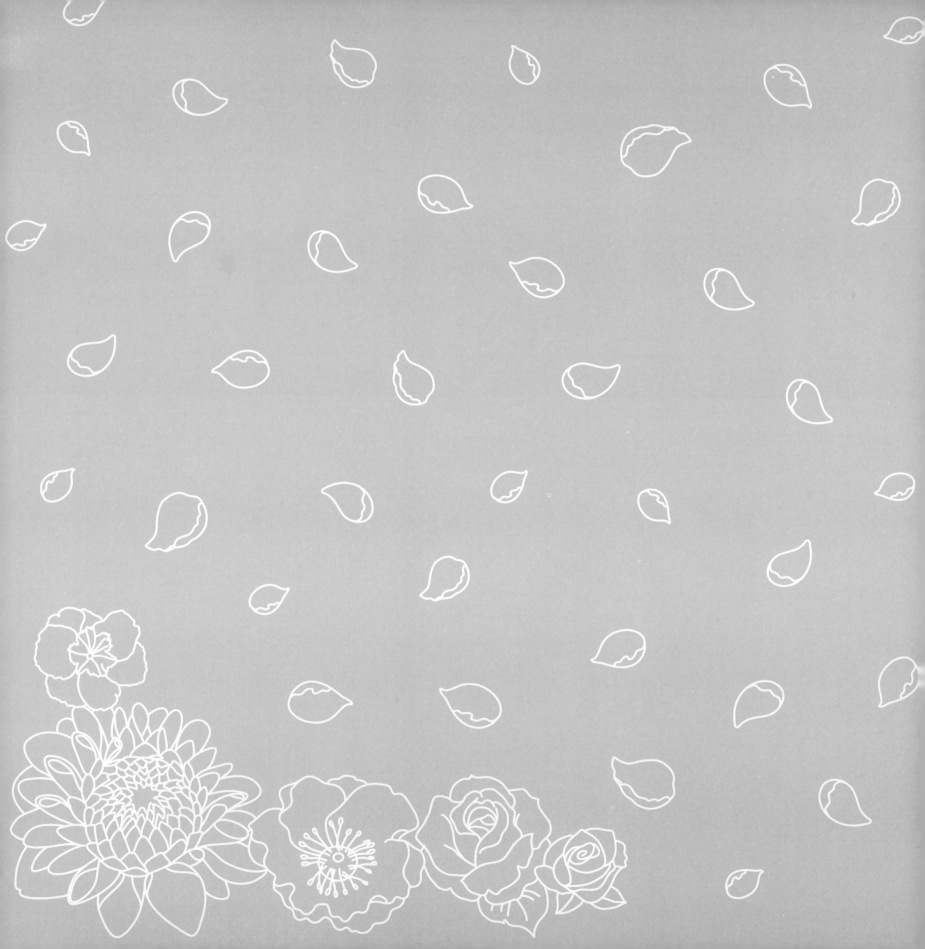

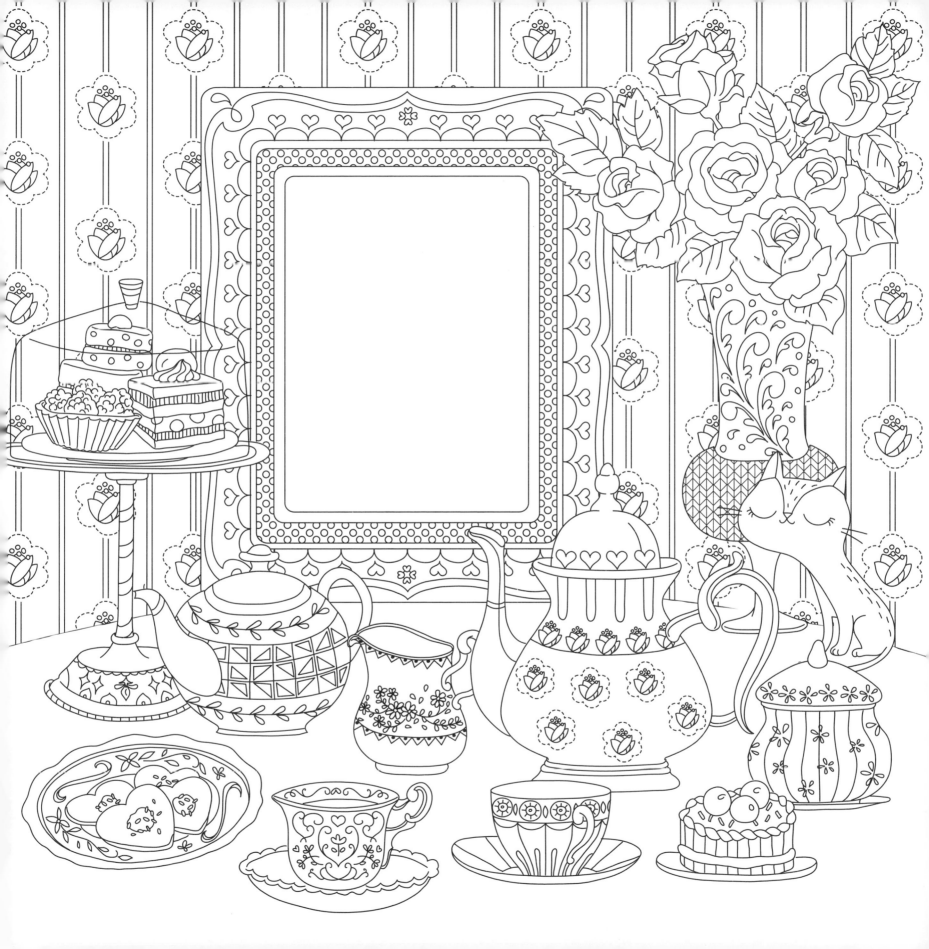

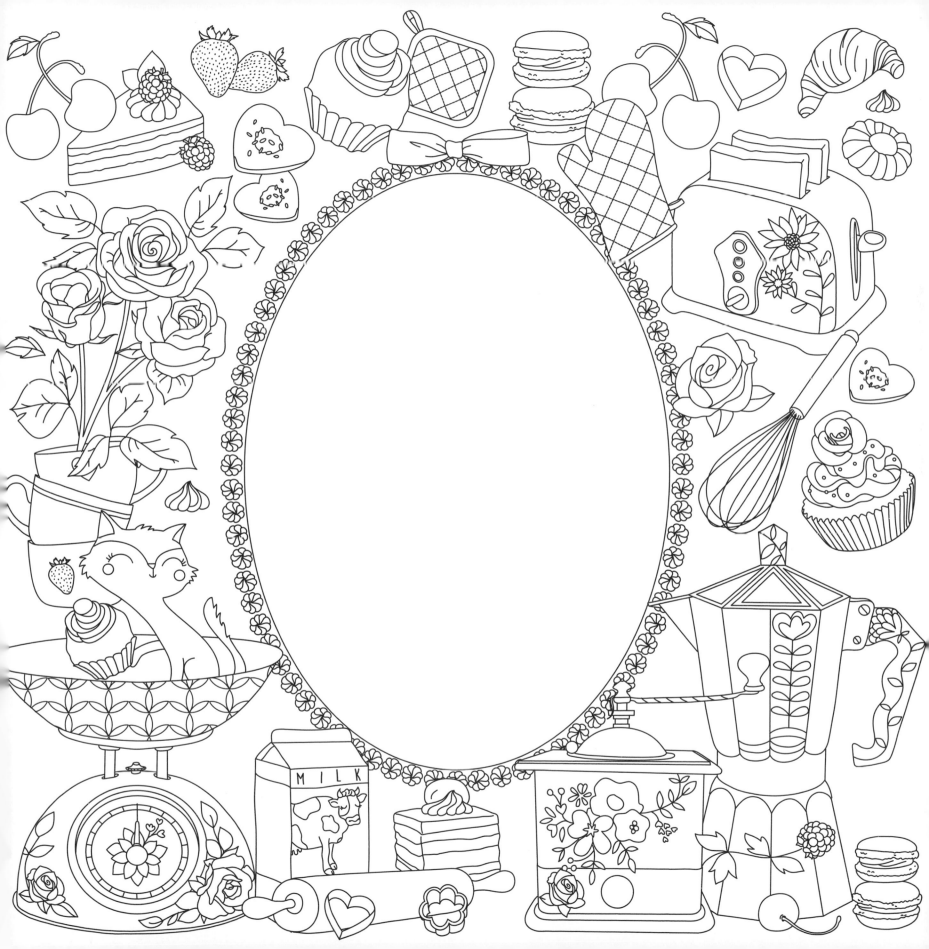

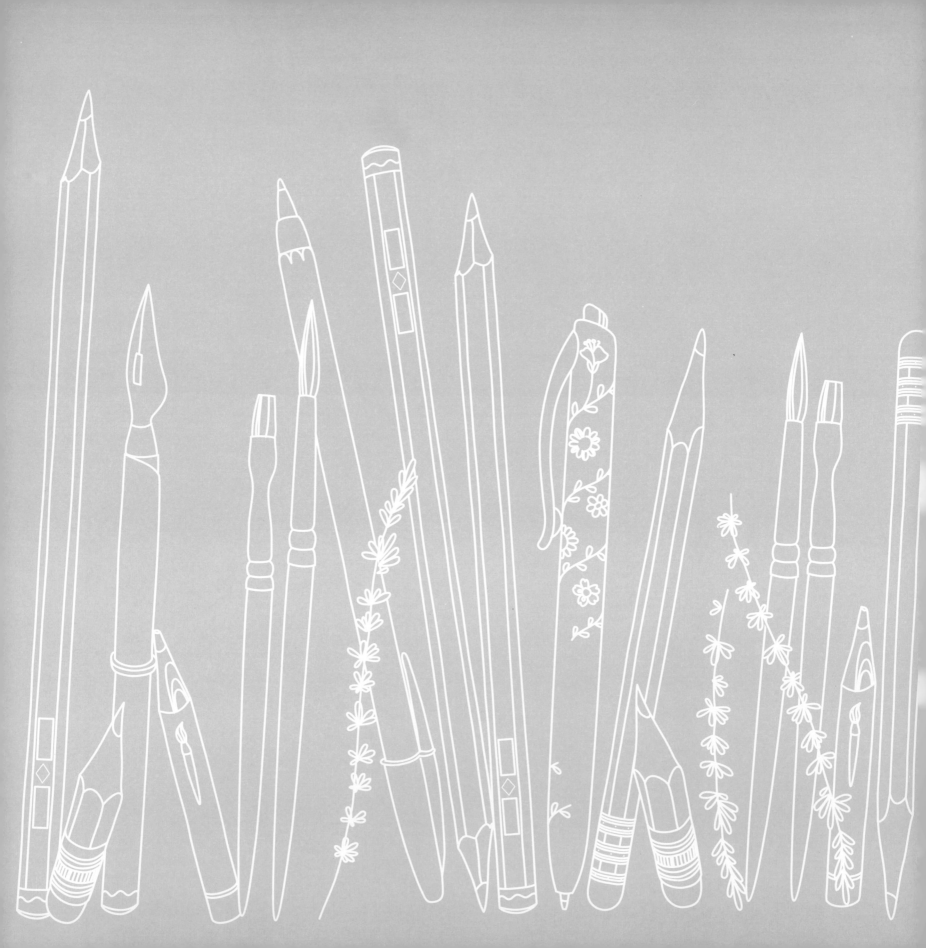

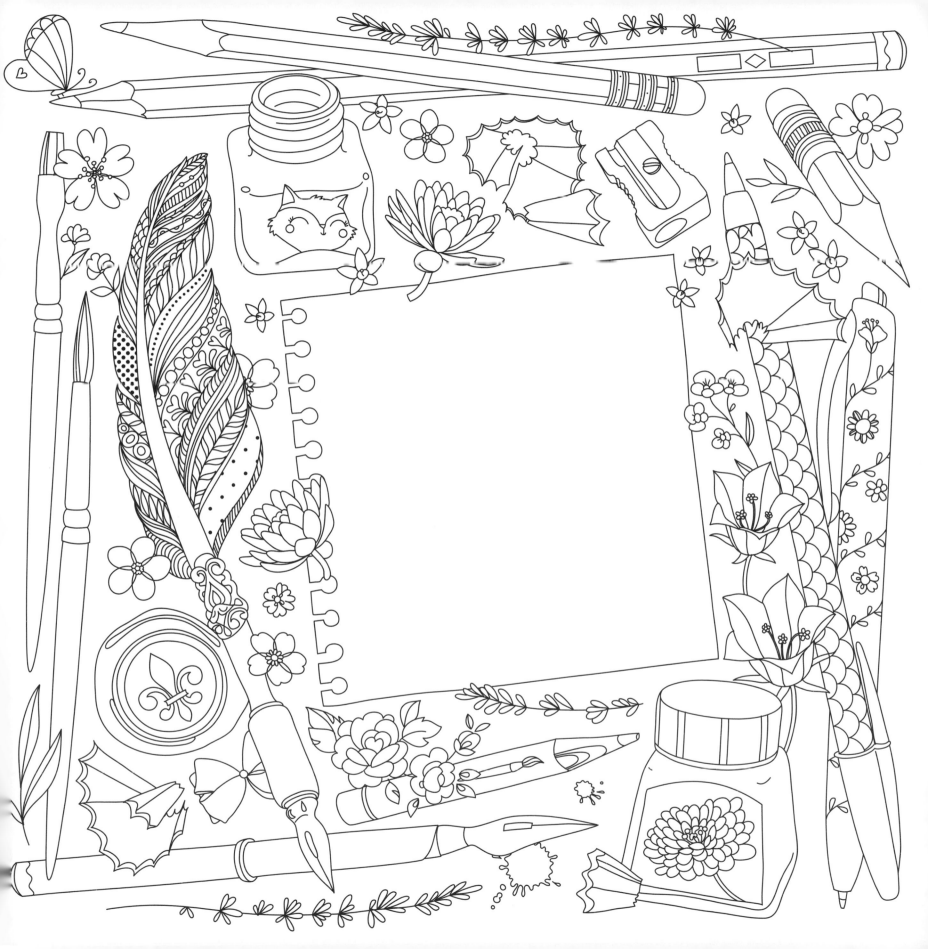

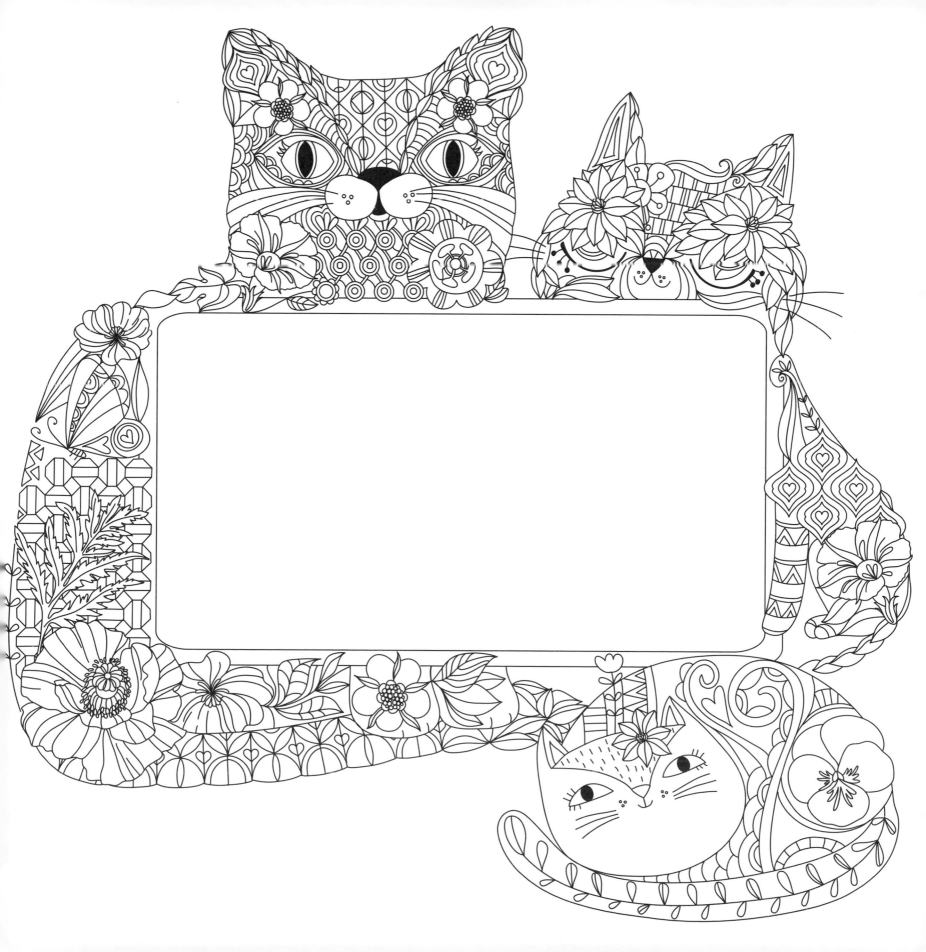

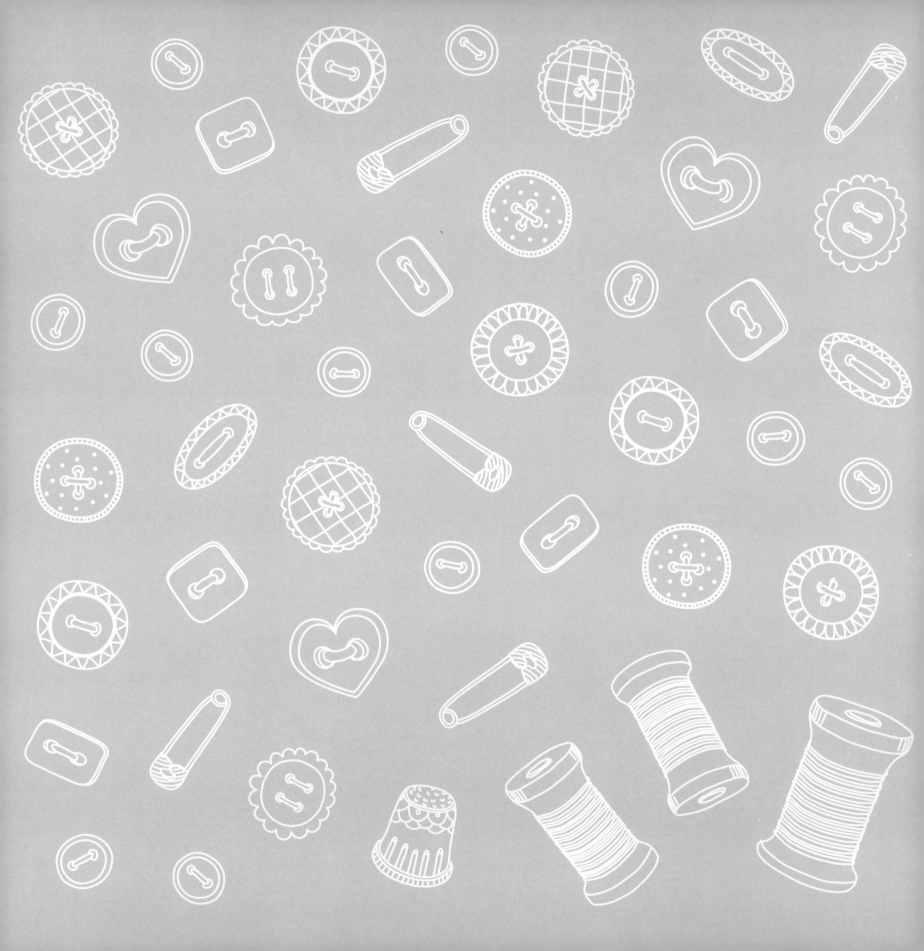

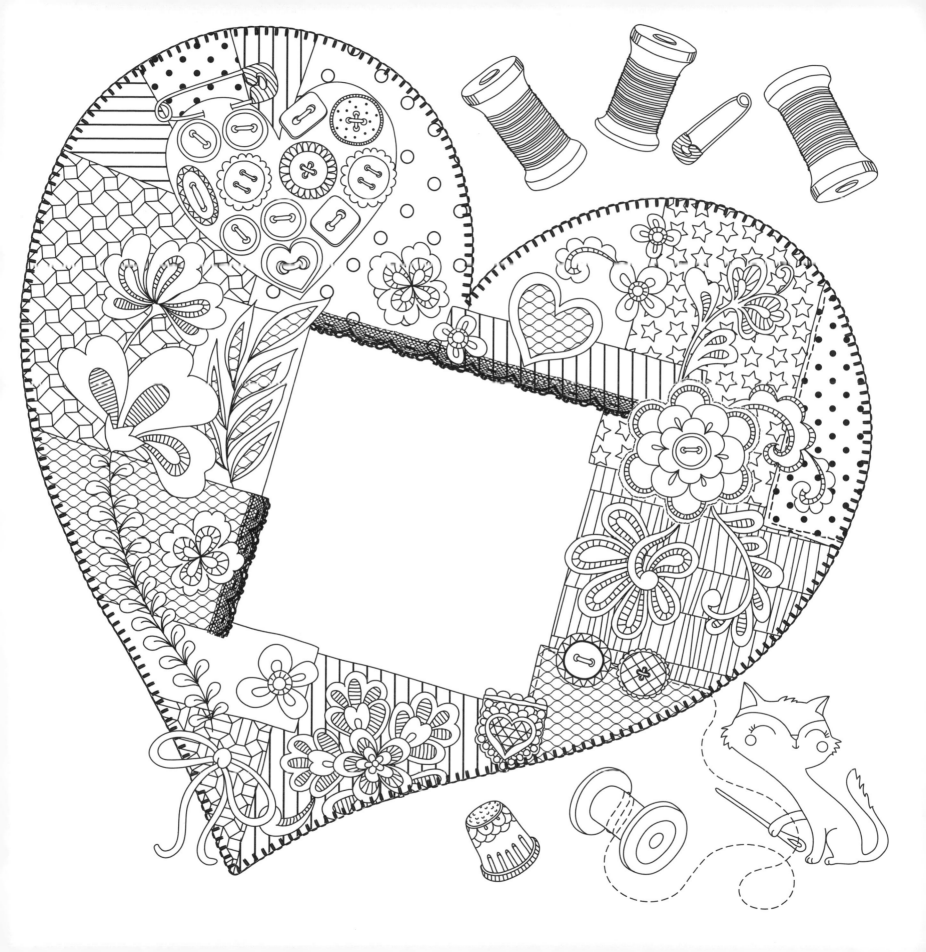

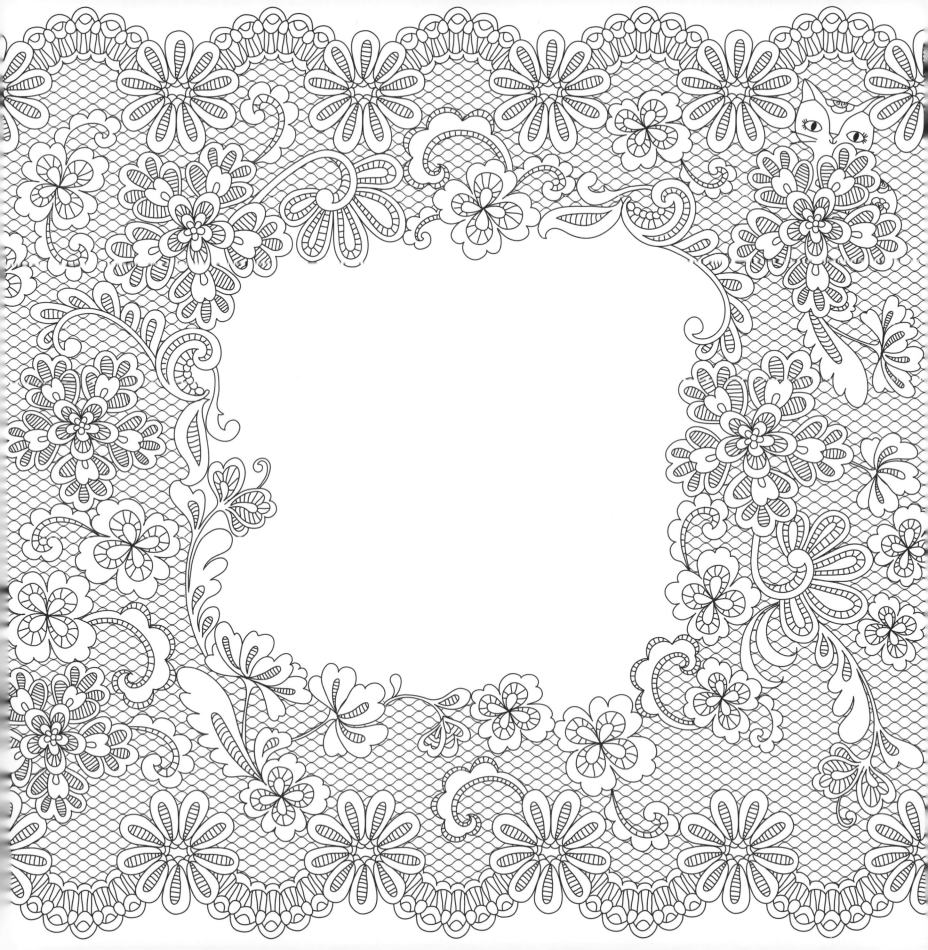

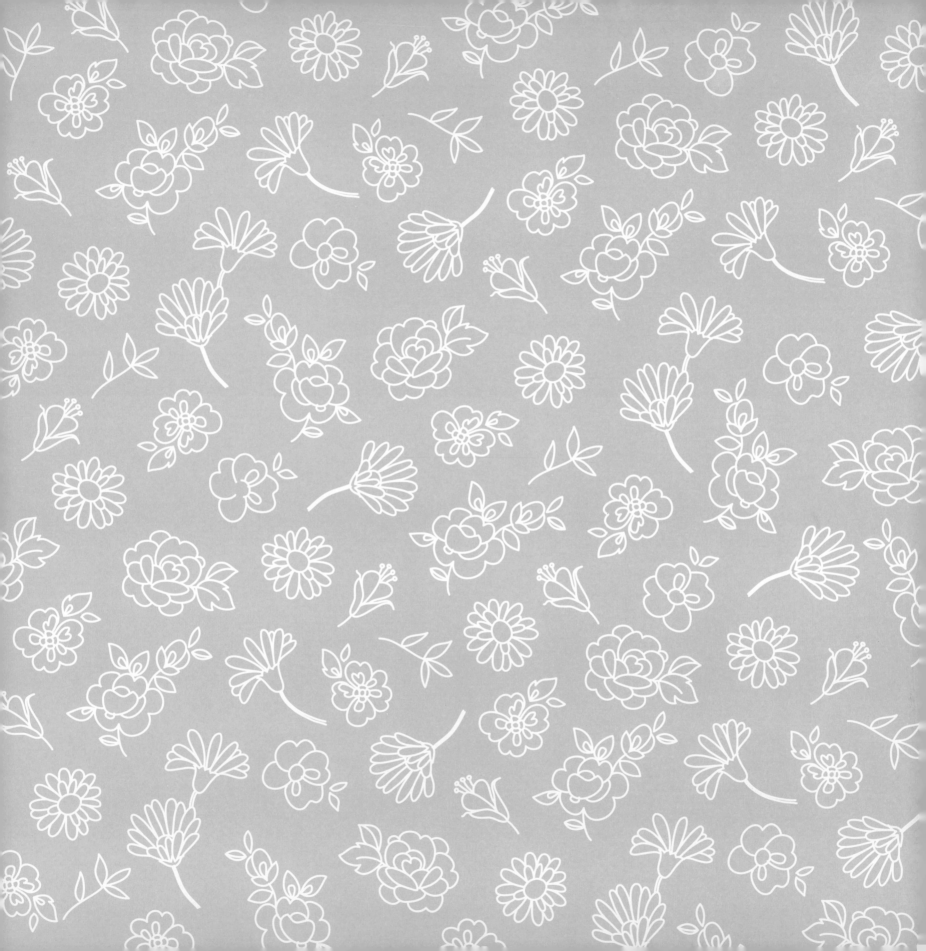

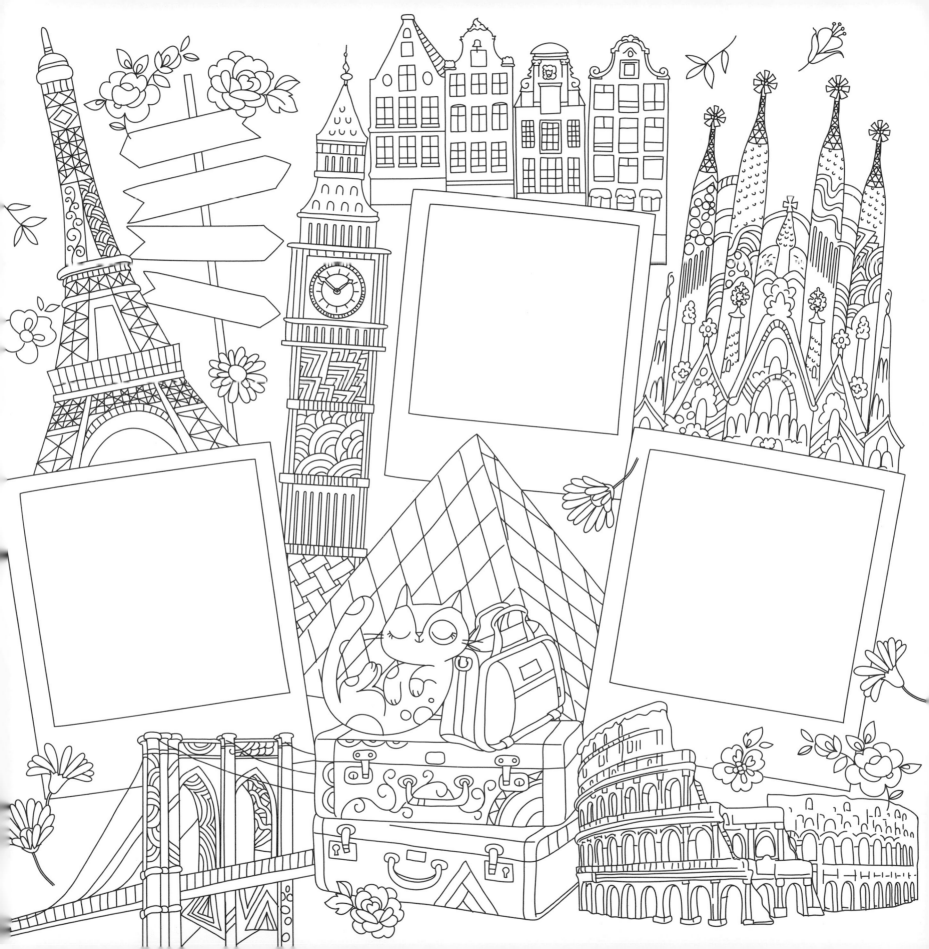

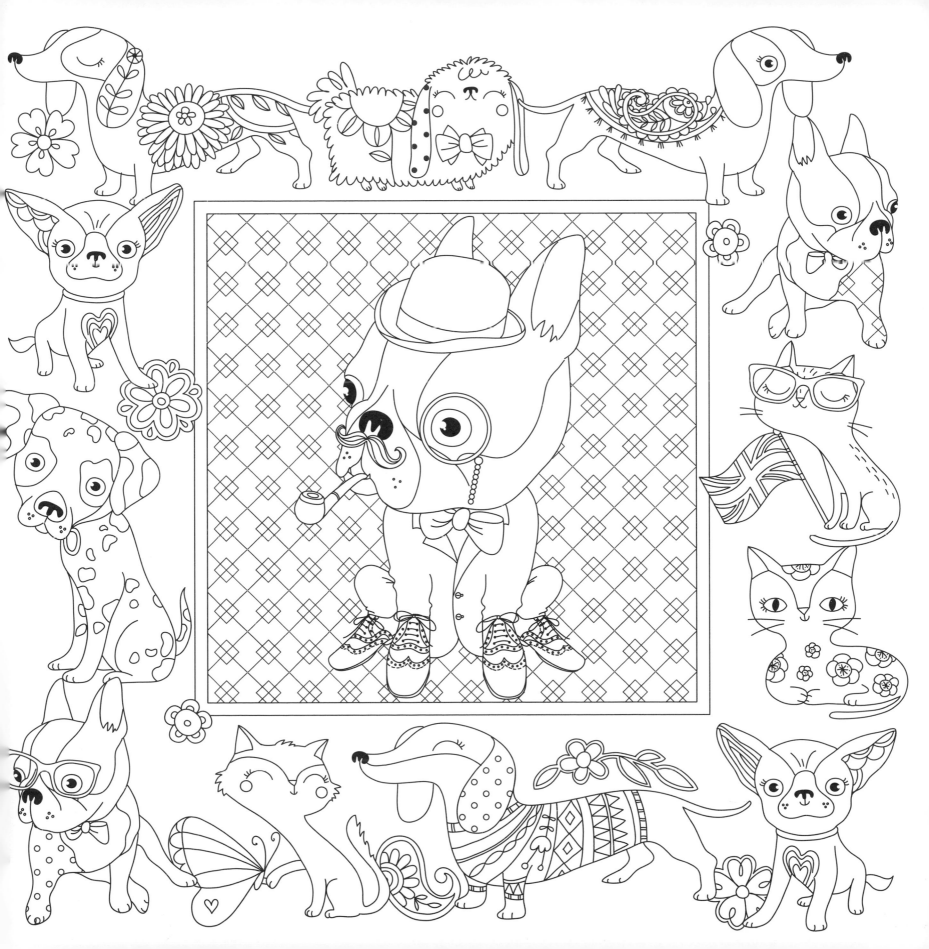

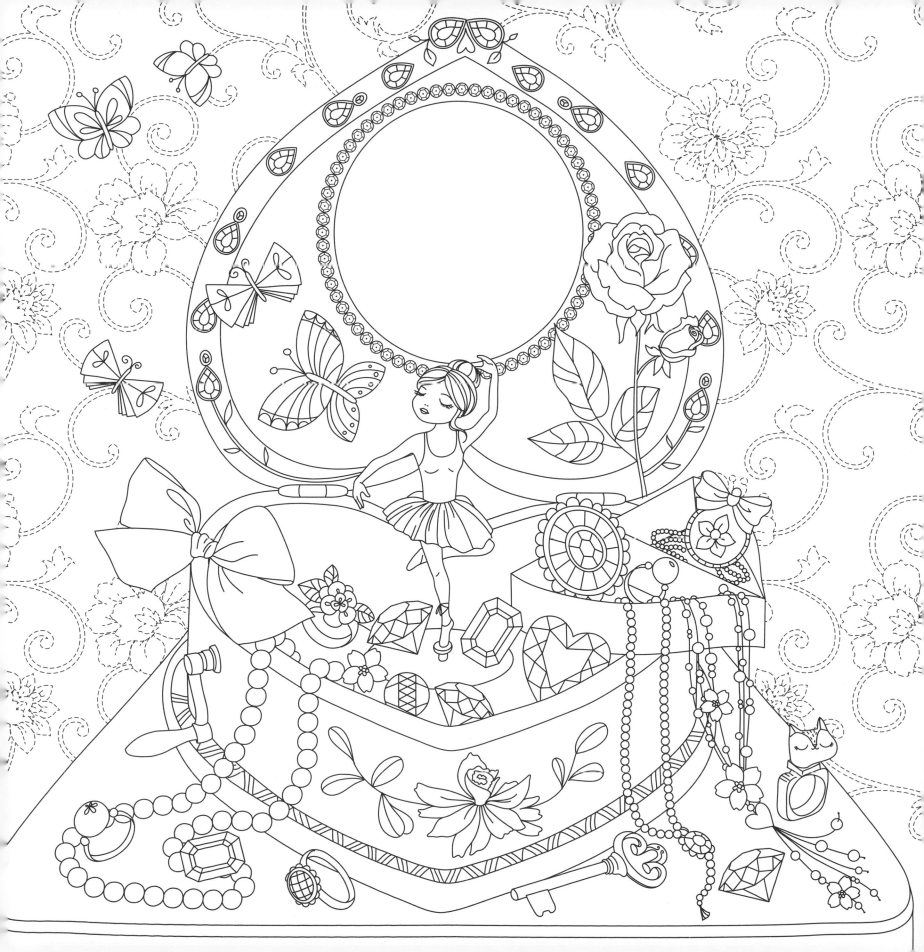

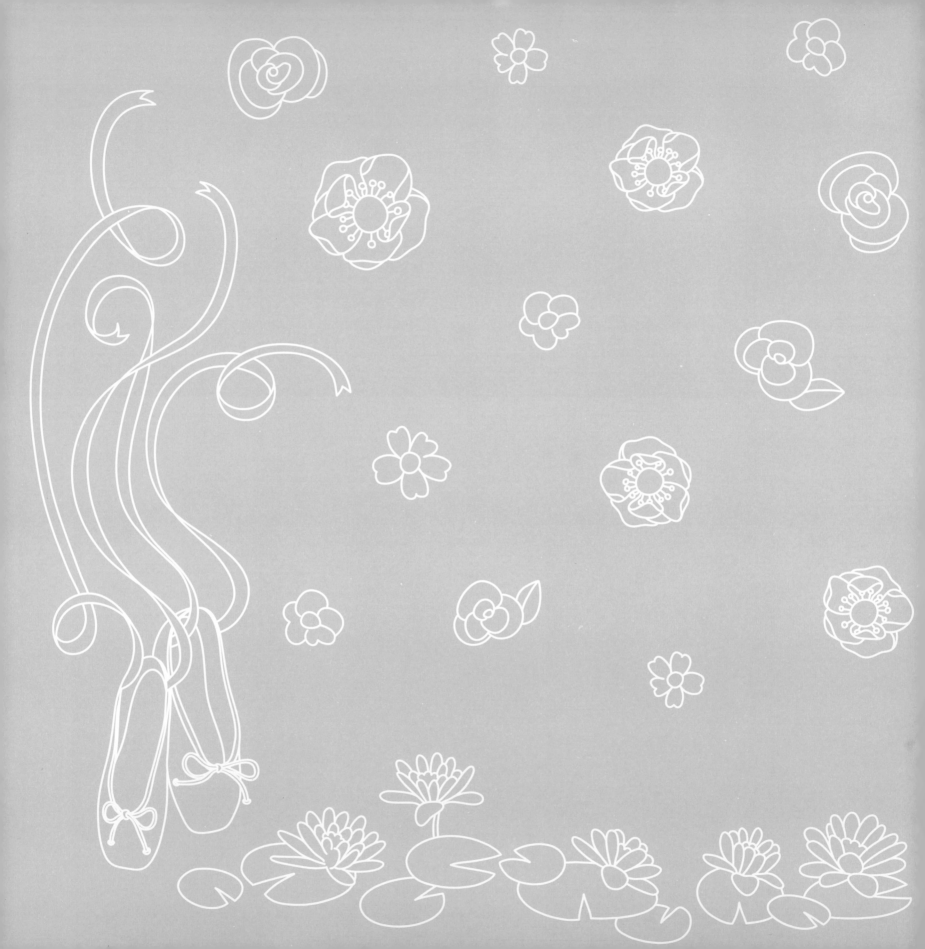

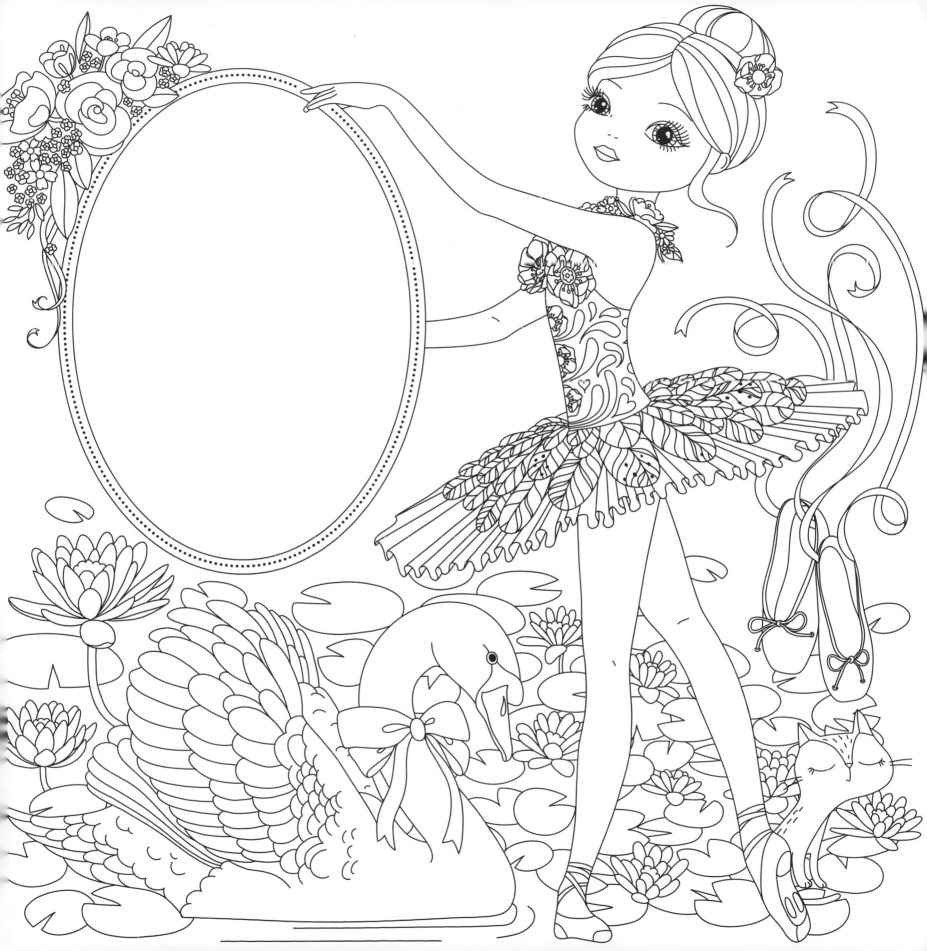

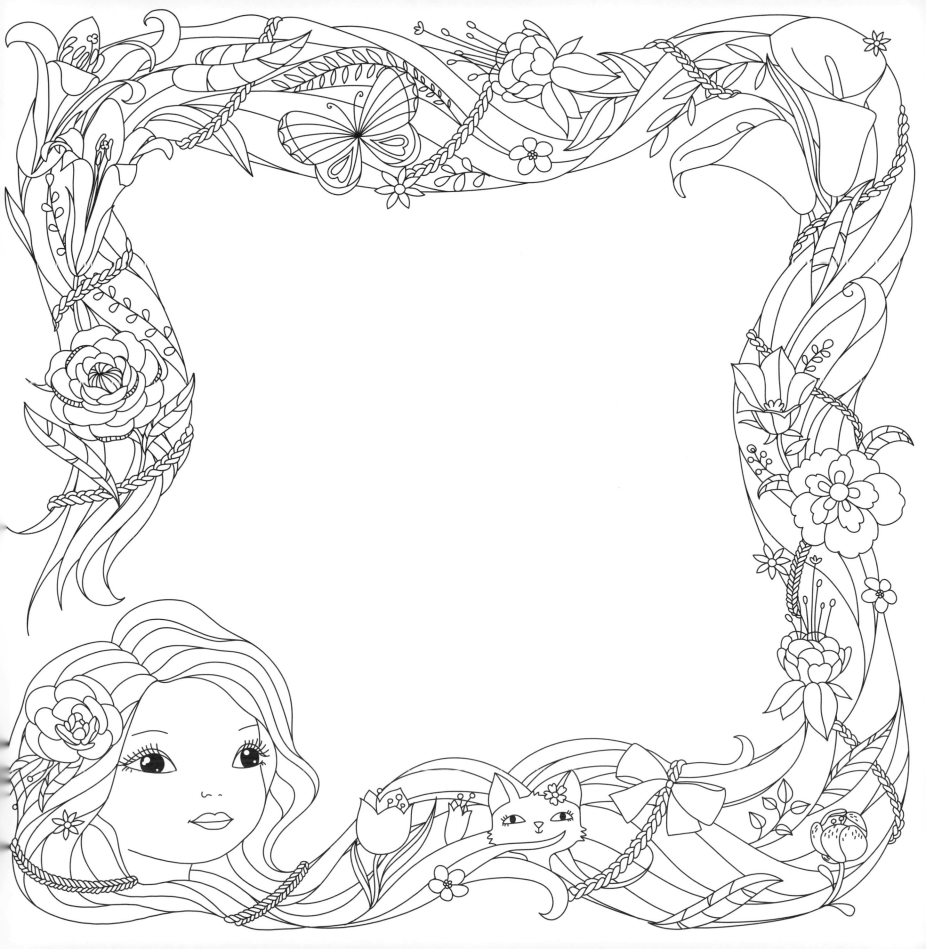

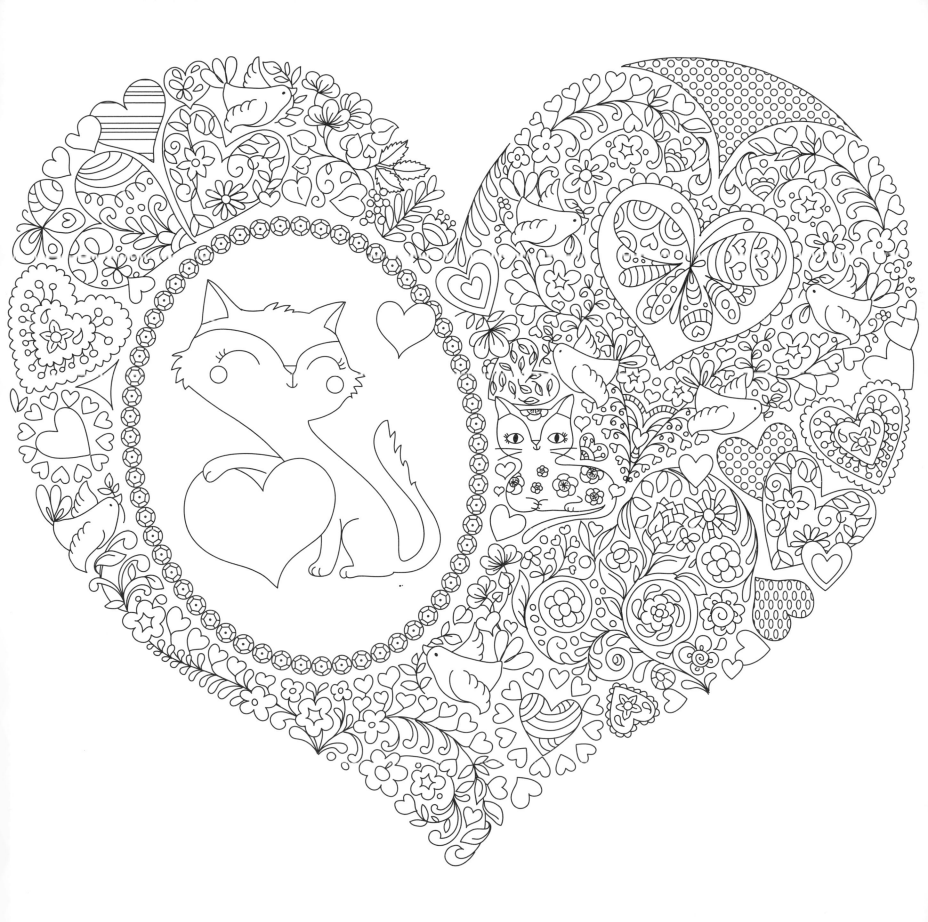

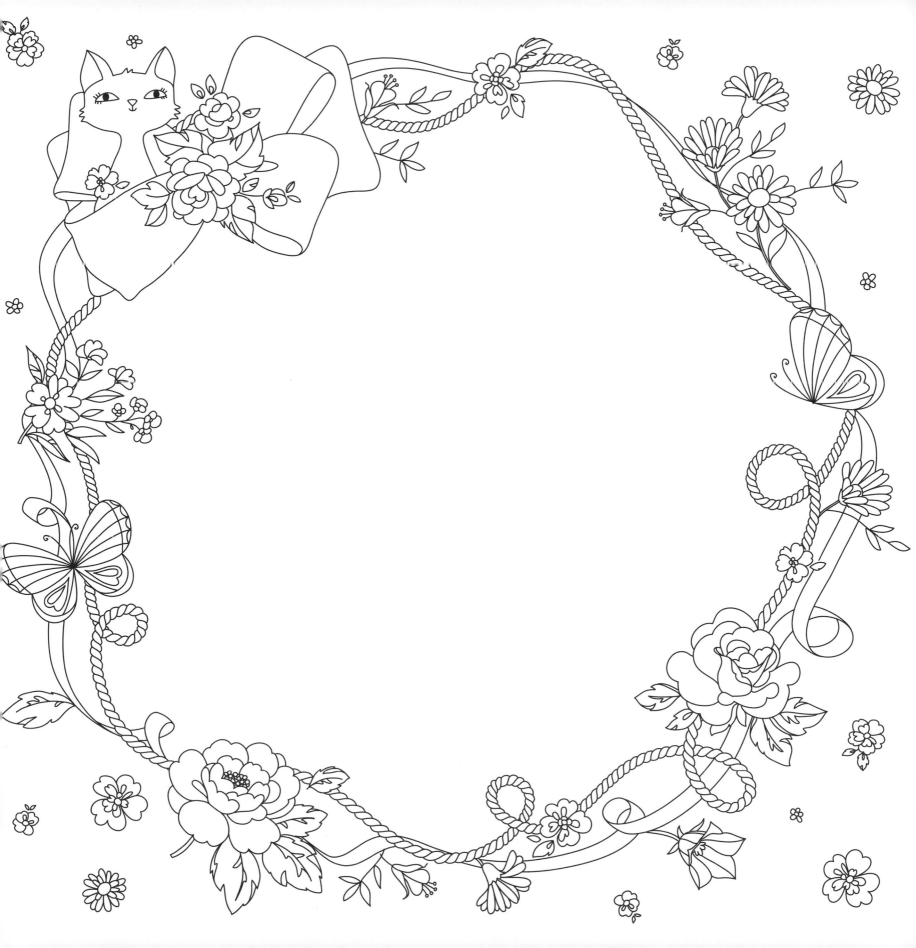

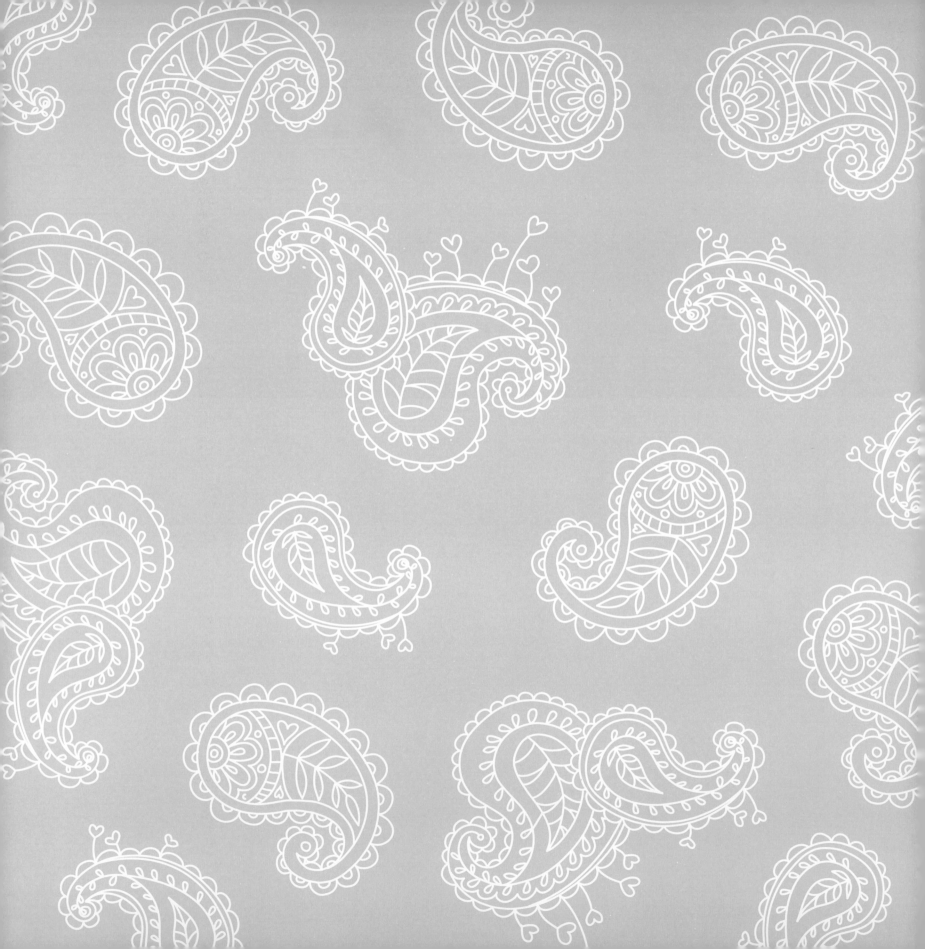

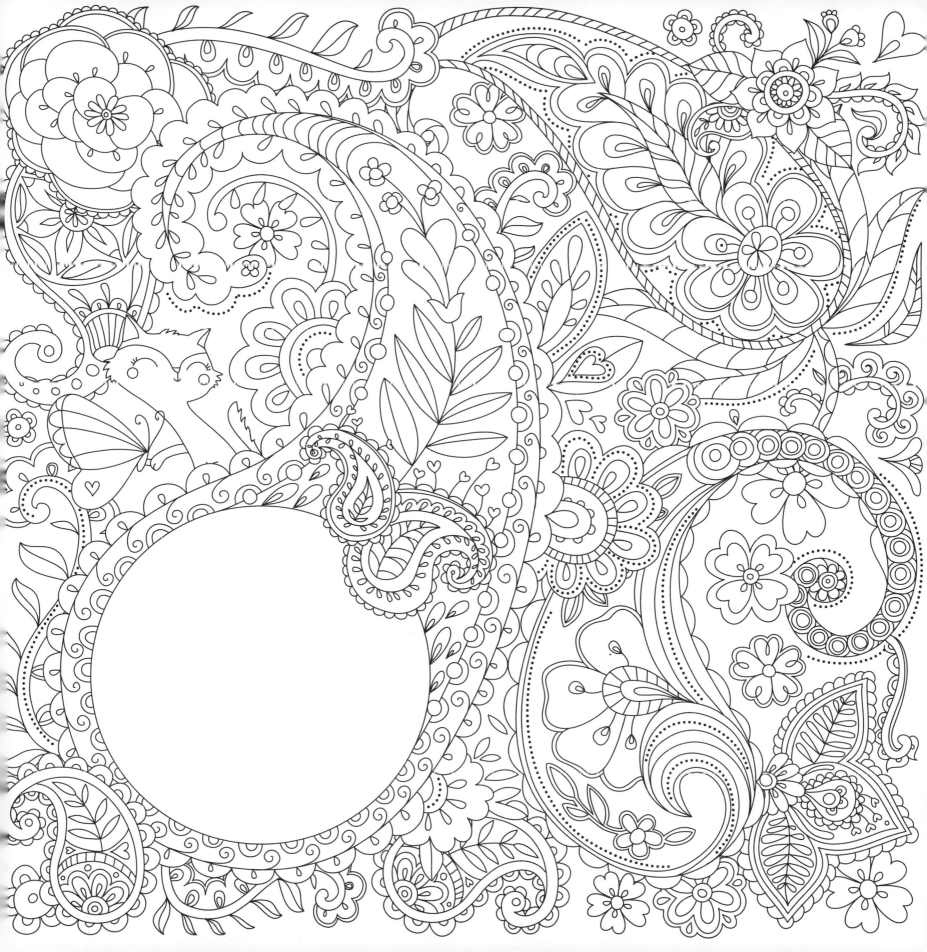

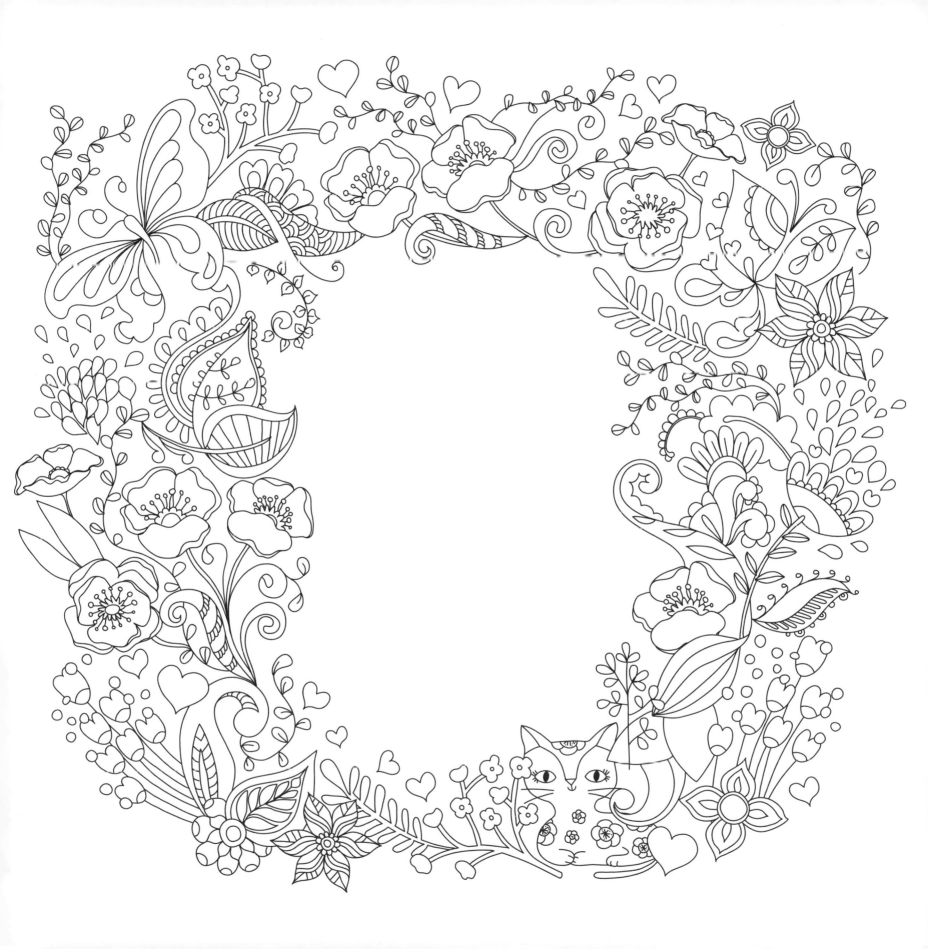

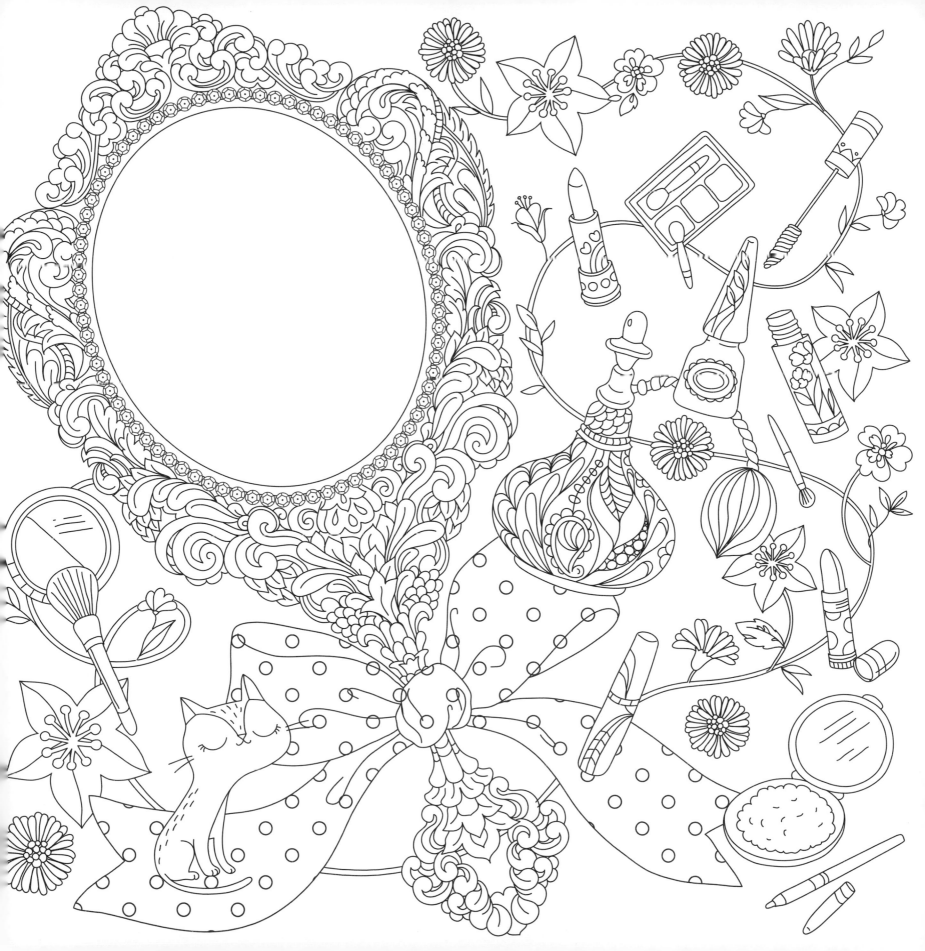

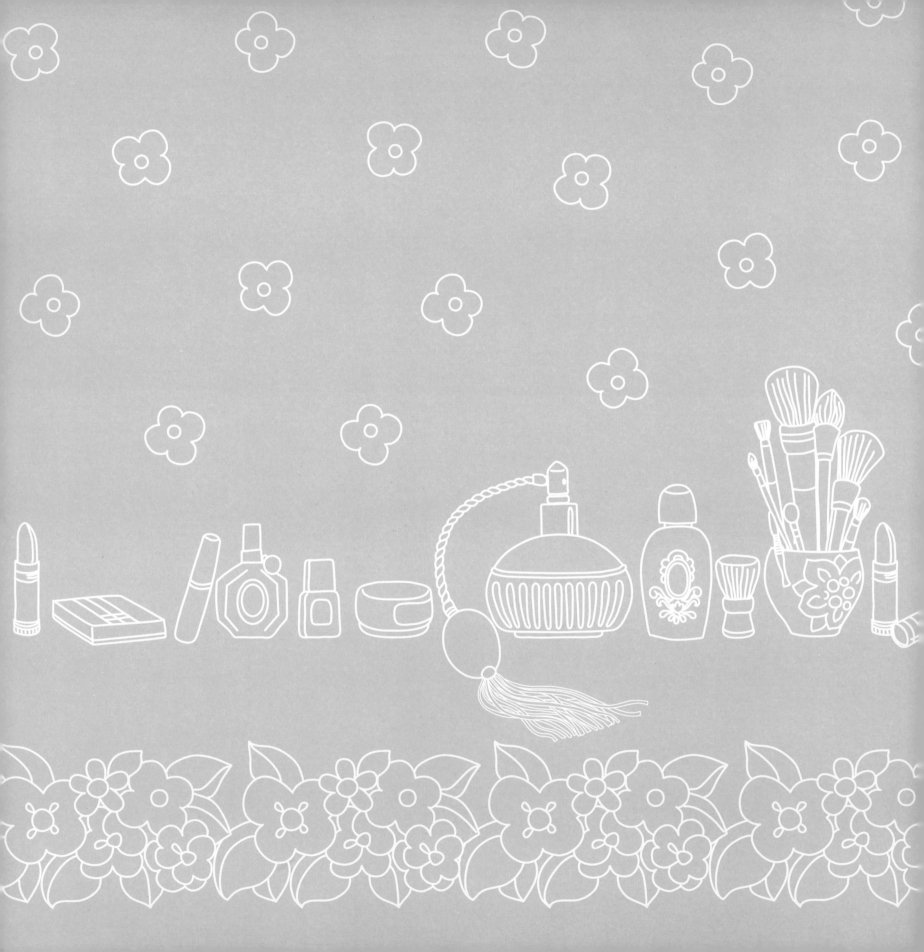

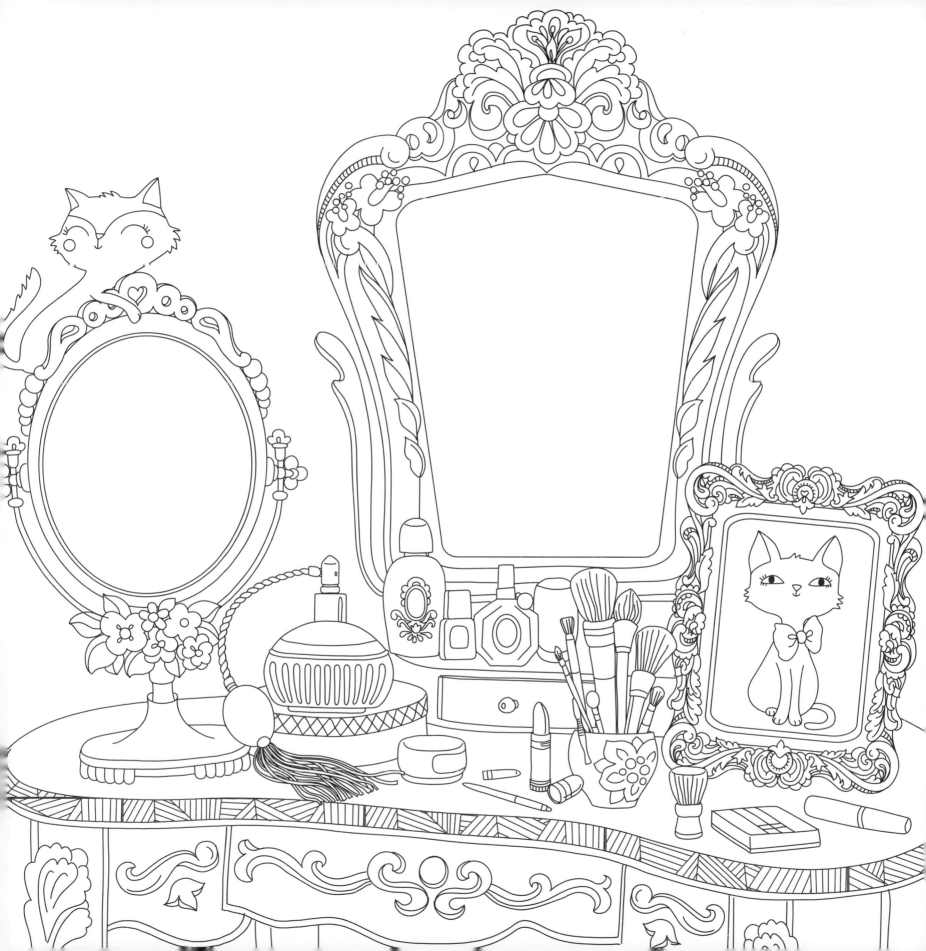

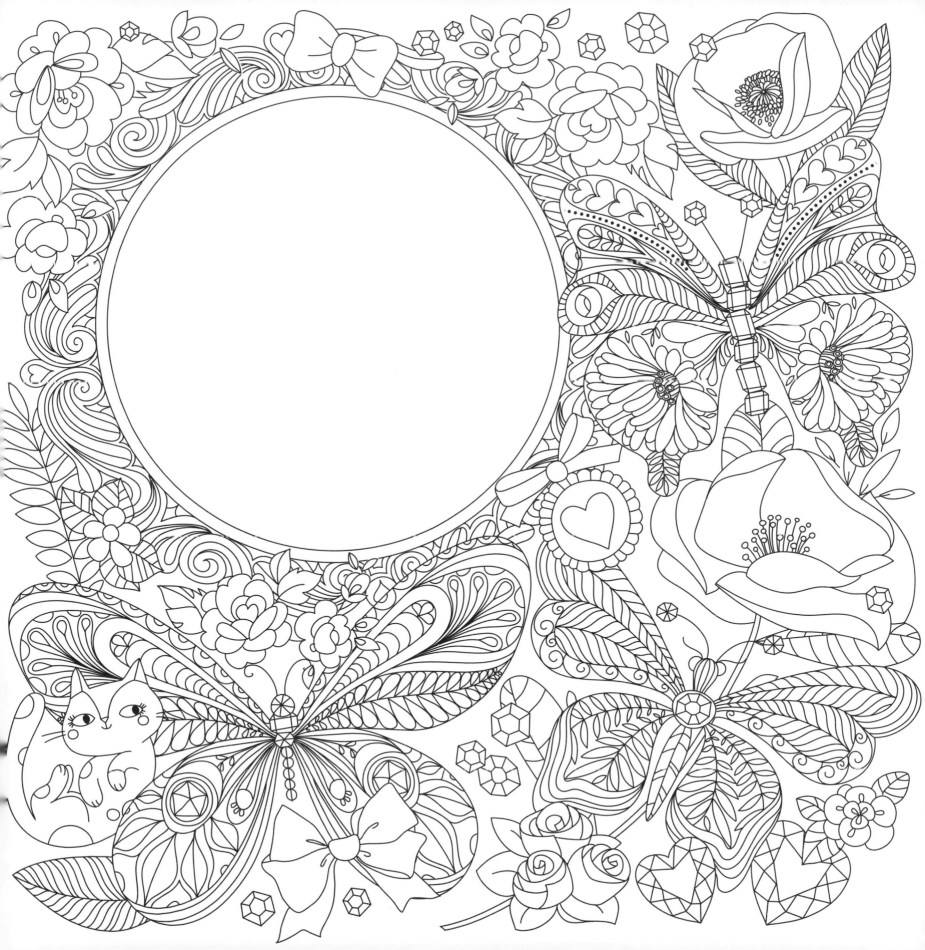

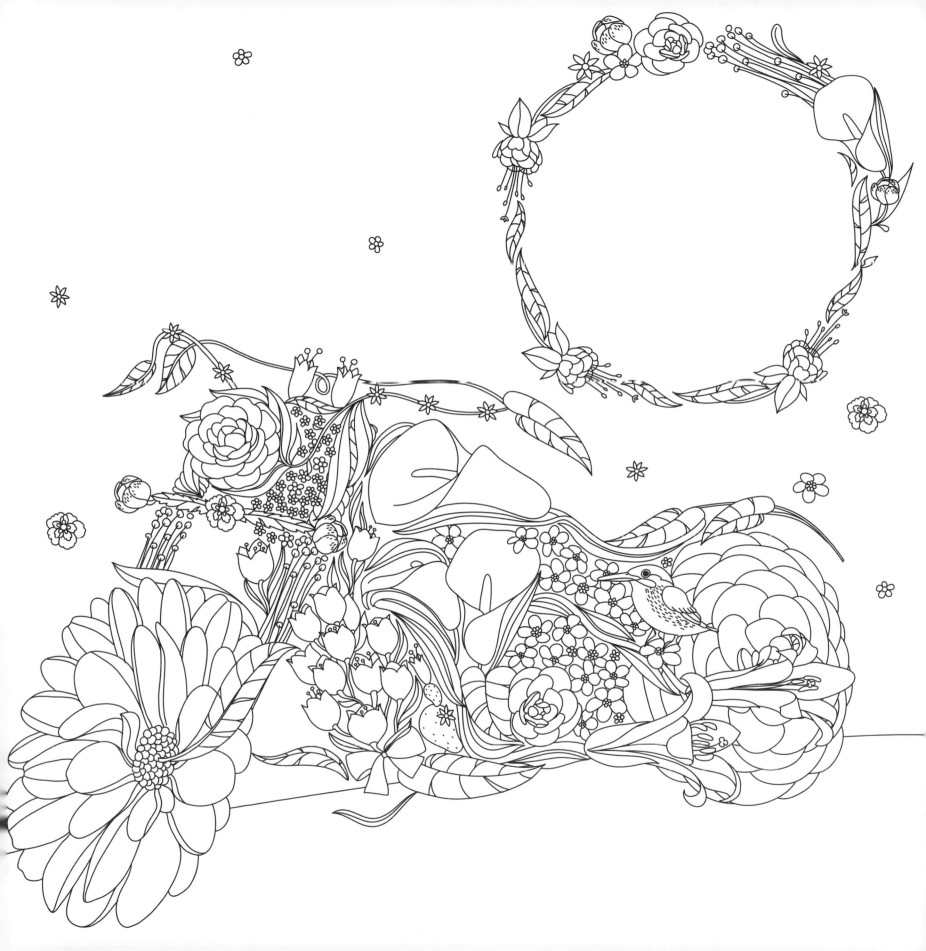

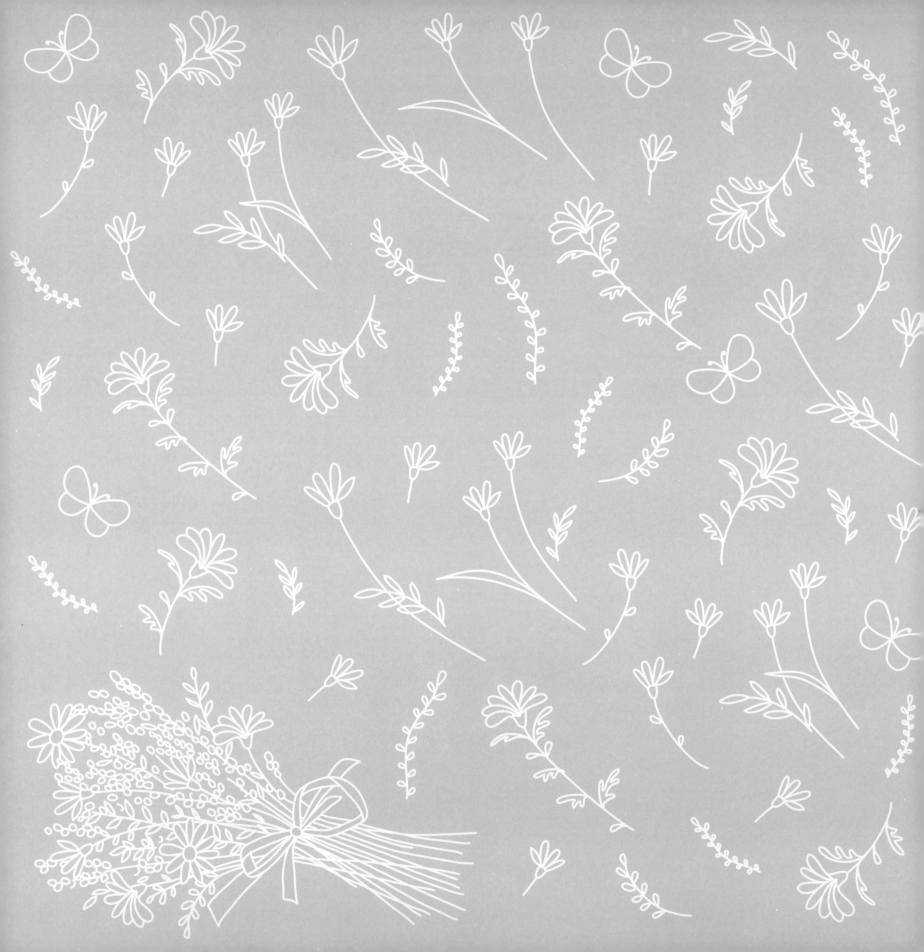

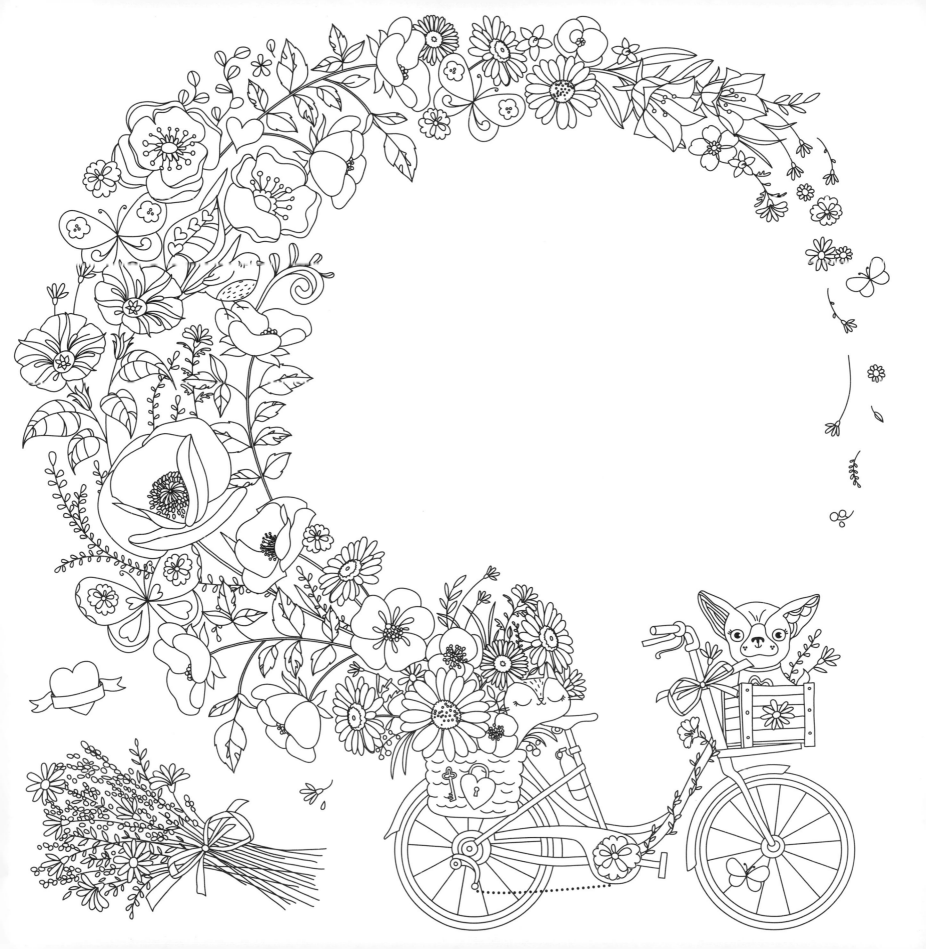

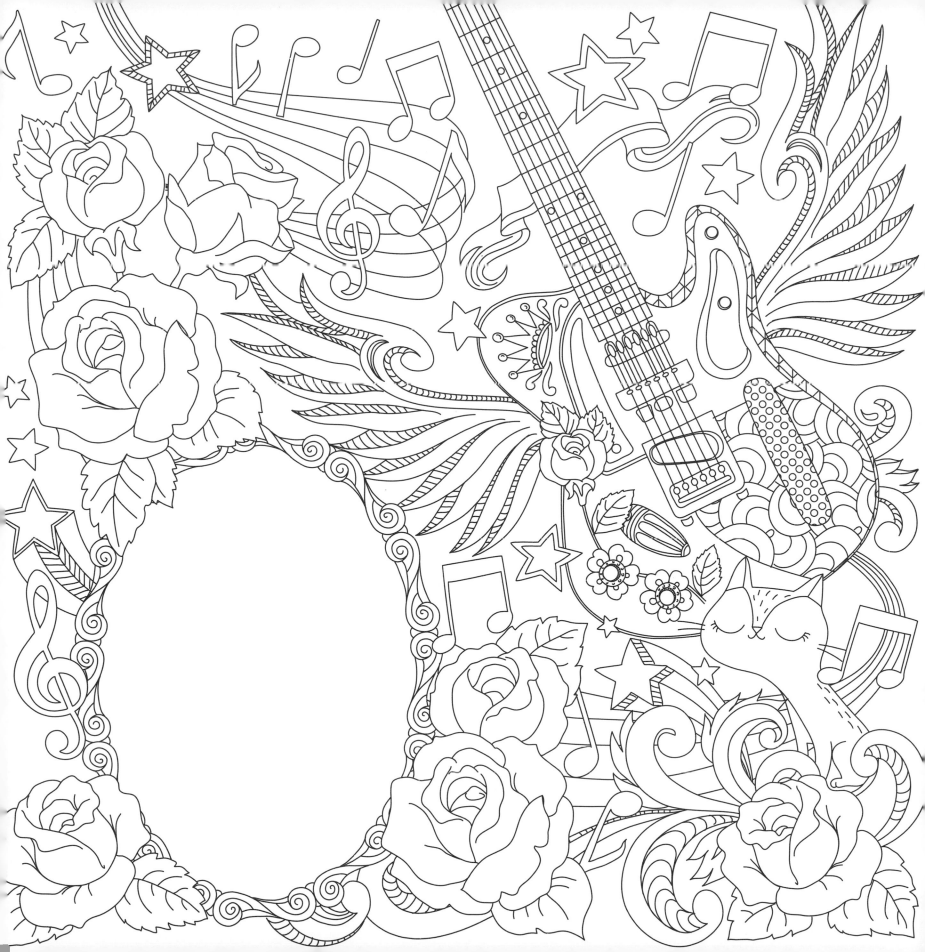

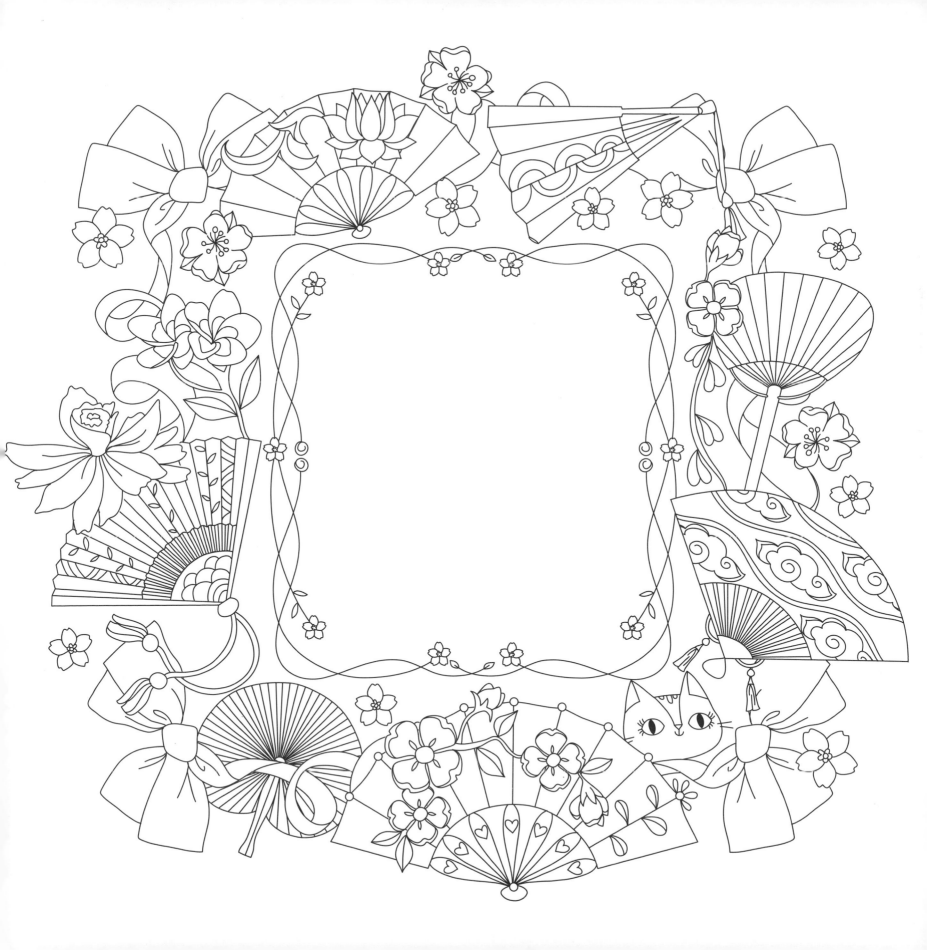

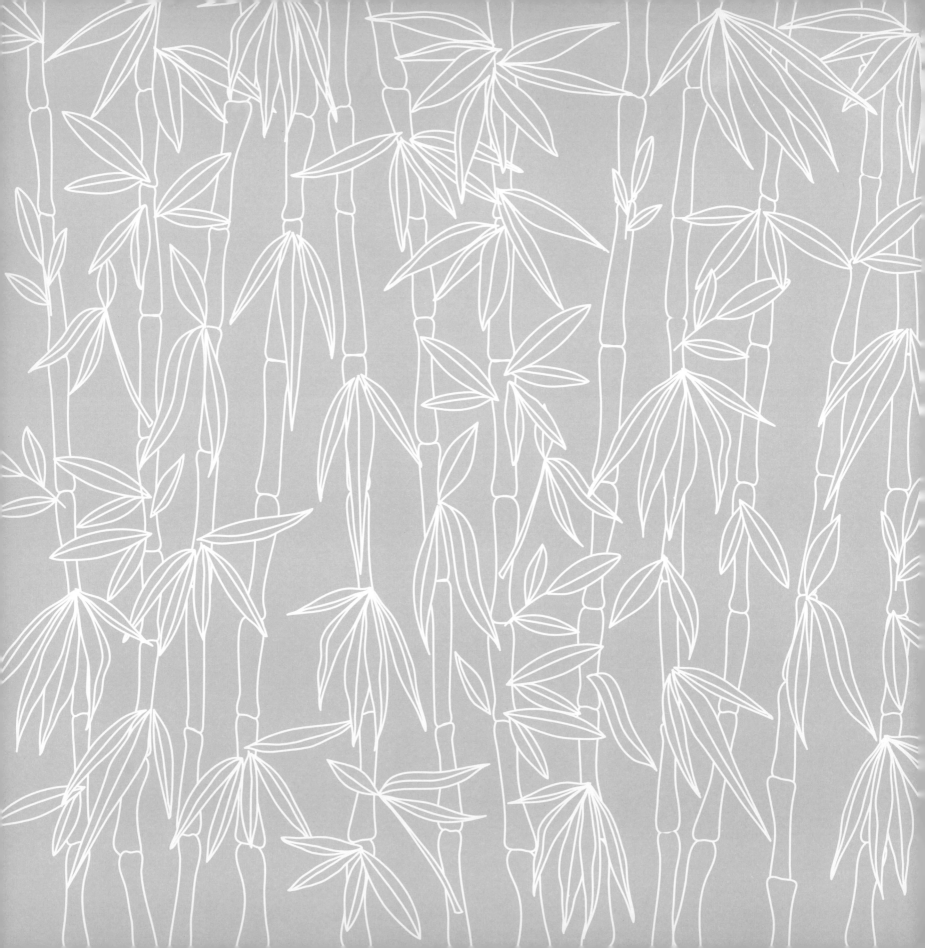

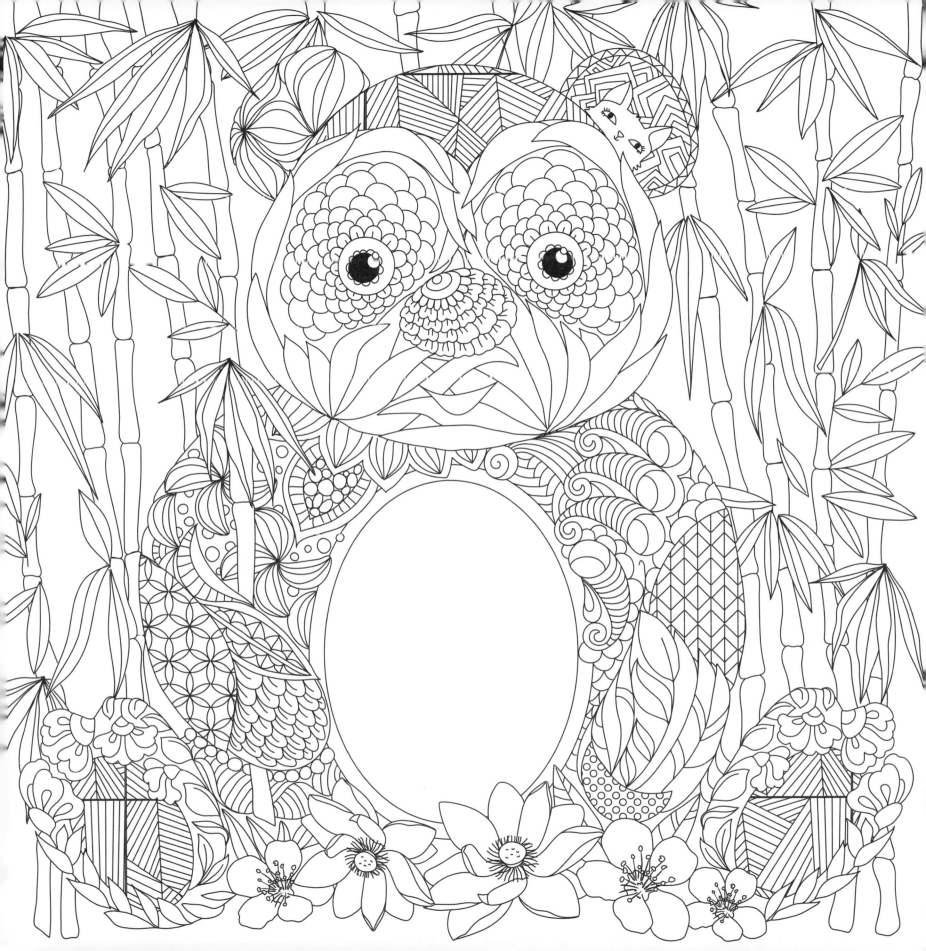

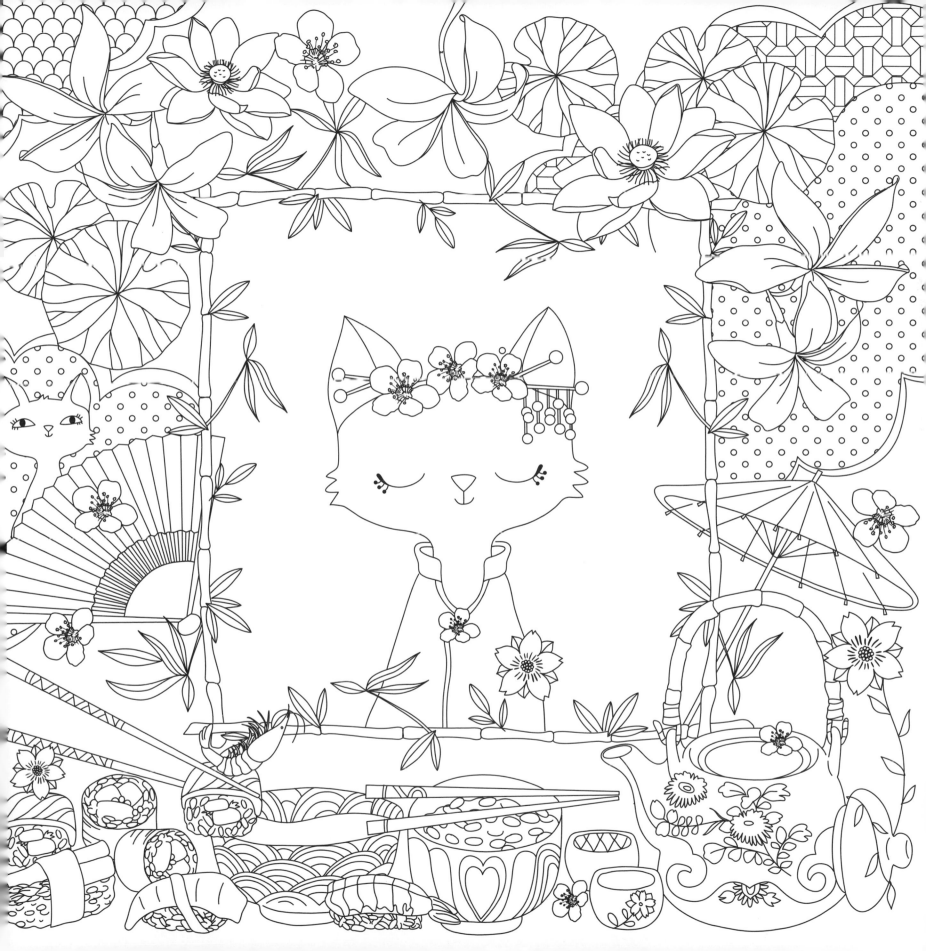

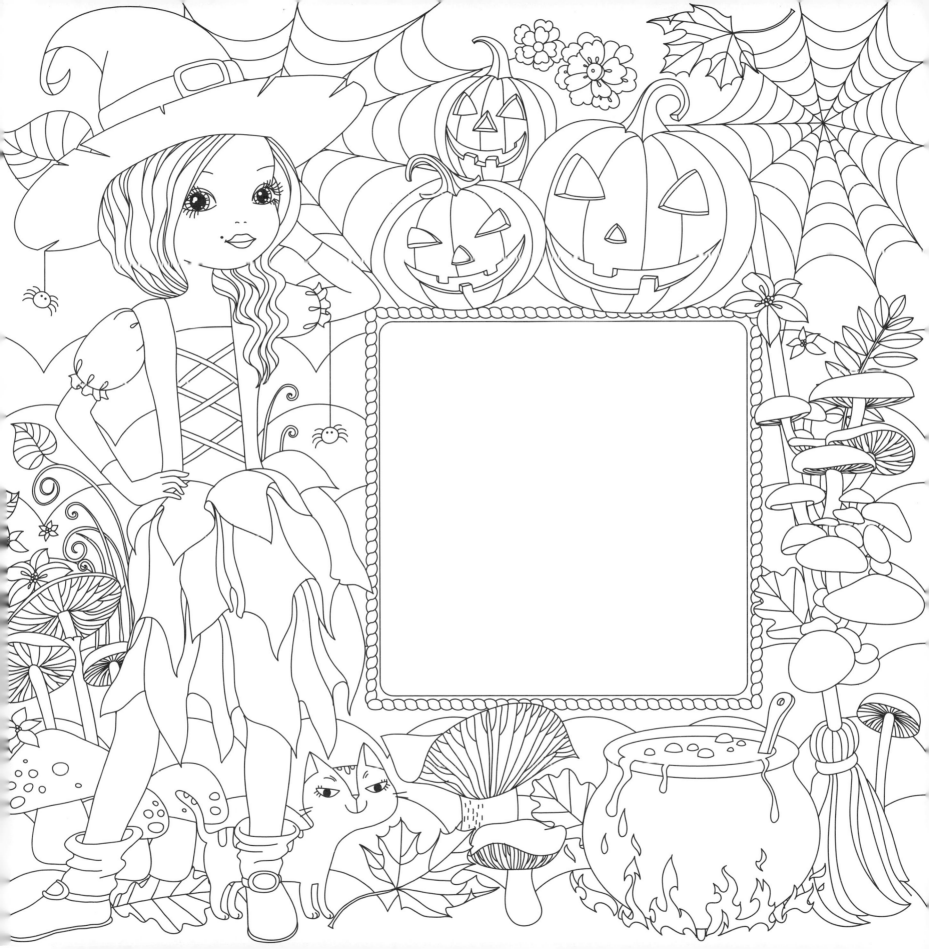

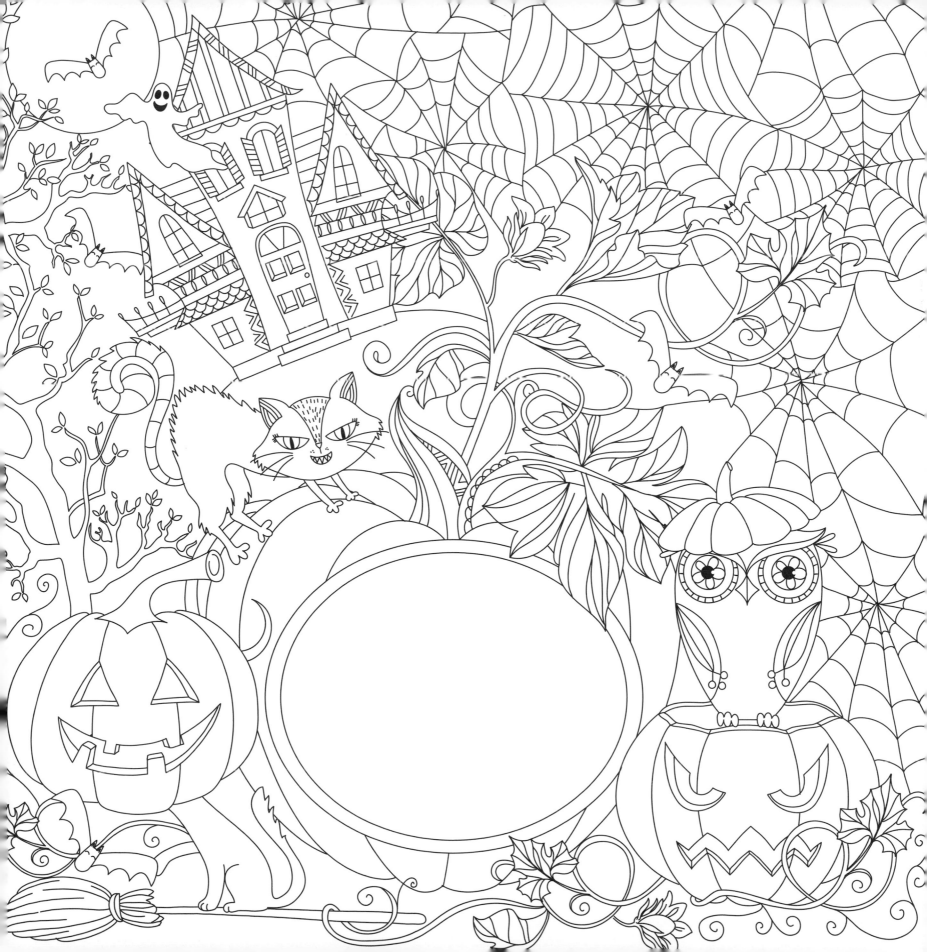

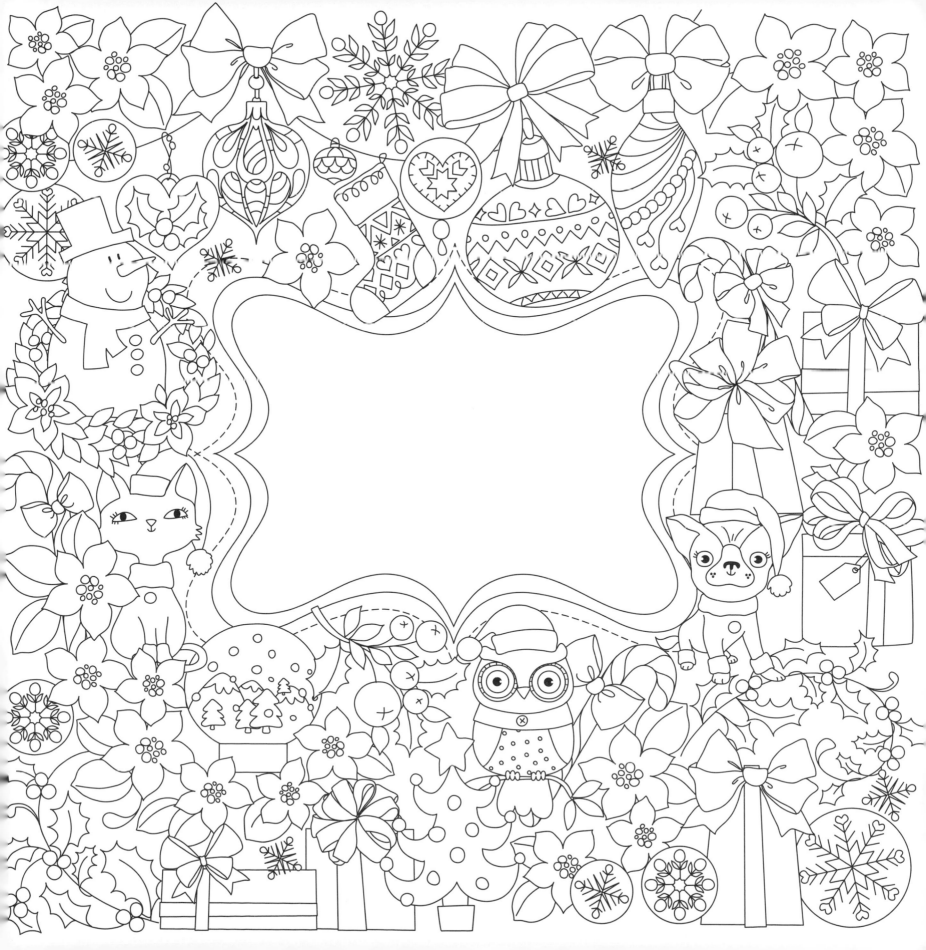

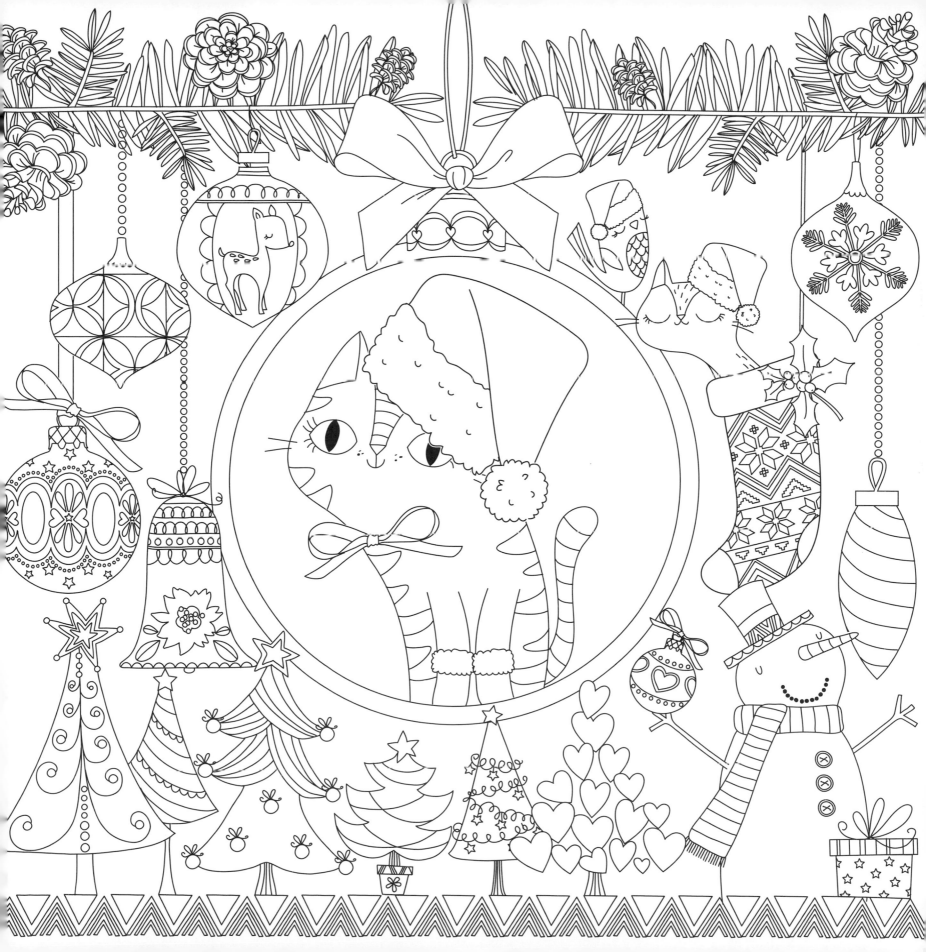

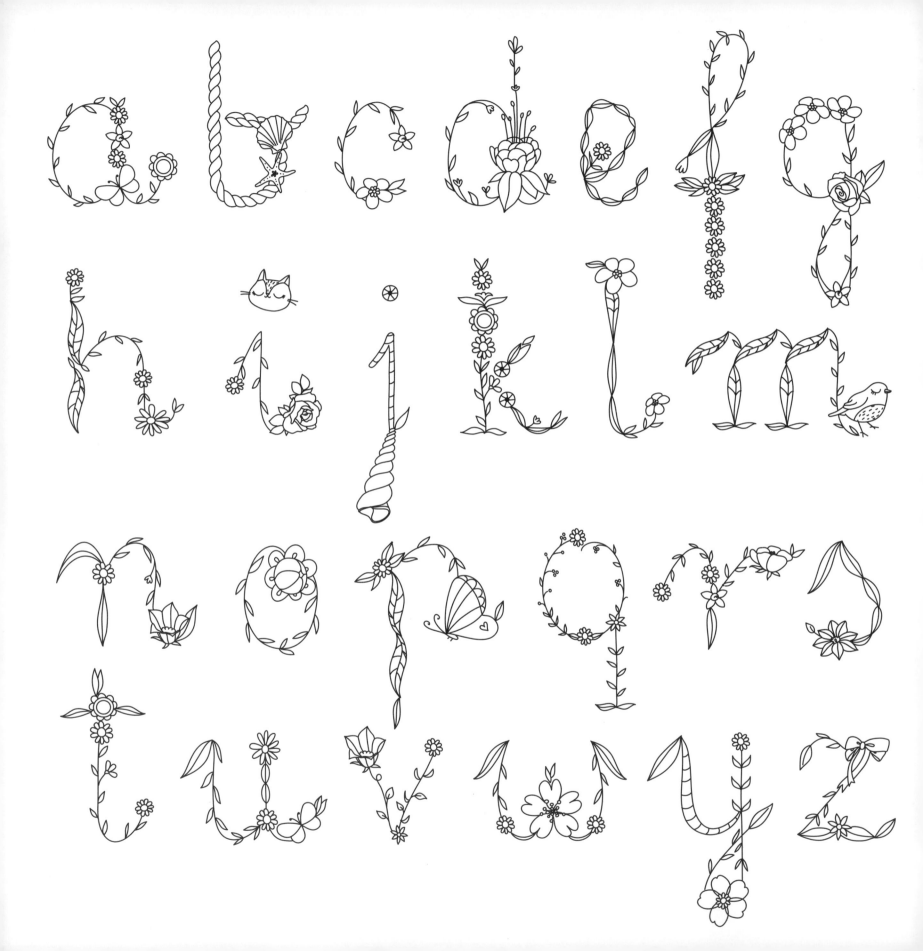

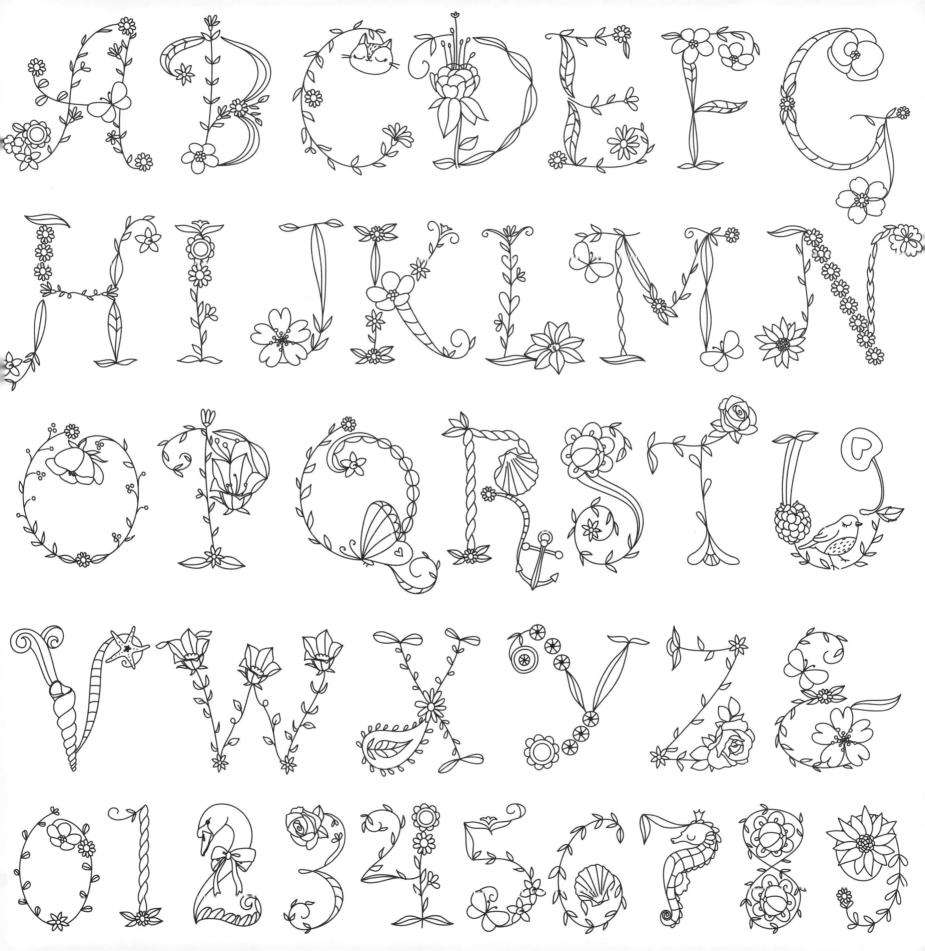

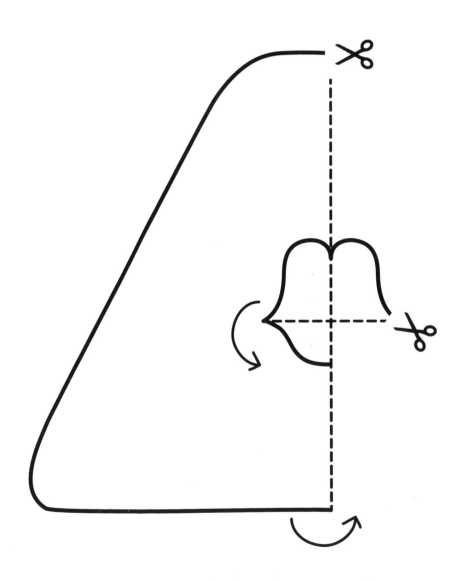

FRAME FANTASIA
A Colouring Book to Keep Your Favourite Moments

MOMENTOS MÁGICOS
Colorea y enmarca tus recuerdos favoritos

MOMENTI MAGICI
Colora e incornicia i tuoi ricordi più belli

NATURE CADRÉE
Cadres à colorier

First published by Promopress in English, Spanish, French and Italian: 2016

© Illustrations: TOC DE GROC

Cover design: Mercè Rocadembosch
Layout: Antonio G. Tomé

ISBN English Edition: 978-84-16504-44-2
ISBN Spanish Edition: 978-84-16504-80-0
ISBN French Edition: 978-84-16504-79-4
ISBN Italian Edition: 978-84-16504-82-4

Copyright © 2016 Promopress
Promopress is a brand of:
Promotora de Prensa Internacional S.A.
C/ Ausiàs Marc, 124
08013 Barcelona, Spain
Phone: +34 93 245 14 64
Fax: +34 93 265 48 83
email: info@promopress.es
www.promopresseditions.com
Facebook: Promopress Editions
Twitter: Promopress Editions @PromopressEd